'Jim Banting has added... debate which now has increasing momentum. Make no mistake, the future of work will create all the opportunities he outlines. Keep it in your back pocket.' Andy Law, founder of the advertising agency, The Law Firm and author of *Open Minds*.

'At last, a writer who has realised that happiness is situated somewhere between having too much and not having enough.' Bob Etherington, sales consultant and author of *Cold Calling for Chickens*.

'Jim Banting's book is, quite simply, inspirational. Beautifully written, it will help you to lead the life you want so that every day leaves you feeling happy, fulfilled and successful.' Simon Tupman, business consultant and author of *Why Entrepreneurs Should Eat Bananas*.

'Persistence is a vital quality but so is knowing when to cut your losses and move on.' Luke Johnson, Chairman, Channel 4 Television and Risk Capital Partners.

'*Get a Dog: Don't Work Like One* provides a sense of perspective and practical guidance from the people who know best: successful senior executives and leaders. Jim Banting delivers a fascinating, insightful and highly practical read – one that will help you succeed in your career in a way that is purposeful, fulfilling and balanced. I urge you to read this book – life is too short not to.' Jeremy Kourdi, management consultant and author of several business books.

'I've been fortunate enough to find balance in my life. I hope others will be inspired to do the same by reading Jim Banting's book. Jim writes in a down-to-earth style that perfectly suits his subject: how to enjoy your work but not be ruled by it, and how to be a happier human being'. Andy Maslen, founder of Sunfish copywriting agency and author of *Write to Sell*.

Get a Dog:
Don't Work Like One

Think differently about
your work-life balance

Jim Banting

Marshall Cavendish
Business

Copyright © 2010 Jim Banting
This paperback edition published in 2010 by Marshall Cavendish Business
An imprint of Marshall Cavendish International
PO Box 65829
London EC1P 1NY
United Kingdom
and
1 New Industrial Road
Singapore 536196
genrefsales@sg.marshallcavendish.com
www.marshallcavendish.com/genref

Marshall Cavendish is a trademark of Times Publishing Limited

Other Marshall Cavendish offices:
Marshall Cavendish International (Asia) Private Limited, 1 New Industrial Road,
Singapore 536196 • Marshall Cavendish Corporation. 99 White Plains Road,
Tarrytown NY 10591-9001, USA • Marshall Cavendish International (Thailand) Co
Ltd. 253 Asoke, 12th Floor, Sukhumvit 21 Road, Klongtoey Nua, Wattana, Bangkok
10110, Thailand • Marshall Cavendish (Malaysia) Sdn Bhd, Times Subang, Lot 46,
Subang Hi-Tech Industrial Park, Batu Tiga, 40000 Shah Alam, Selangor Darul
Ehsan, Malaysia

The right of Jim Banting to be identified as the author of this work has been asserted
by him in accordance with the Copyright, Designs and Patents Act 1988.

The author and publisher have used their best efforts in preparing this book and disclaim
liability arising directly and indirectly from the use and application of this book.

All reasonable efforts have been made to obtain necessary copyright permissions.
Any omissions or errors are unintentional and will, if brought to the attention of
the publisher, be corrected in future printings.

A CIP record for this book is available from the British Library

Printed and bound in Singapore by Times Printers Pte Ltd

Contents

Dedication and Acknowledgements

I would like to dedicate this book to all the people I have met along the way. It's been a great adventure and I wish everyone success and happiness, whatever that means in your world. If this book helps just one person on a single occasion, it will have been worth the long hours of toil.

In writing this book I have made every effort to ensure accuracy but any errors that remain are down to my rather less-than-precise memory of incidents and conversations. I would like to thank all those who have helped me assemble the series of ideas and experiences that form the basis of this book into something that is half legible. What follows constitutes a great amount of my heart and soul, and like most good things in life, could not have been done alone. I won't create a long list of all those who have helped; you know who you are.

Writing something like this does provide a marvellous opportunity to sit back and reflect on what success has, and indeed, still does mean to me. I have come to the conclusion that being honest to my ideals, being myself at all times and trying my utmost, will always be strong pillars of my particular existence.

If you have any comments about your work-life experiences or have something you think I could help with, just email me on jimbanting@gmail.com or visit my website www.jimbanting.com.

Good luck with your journey!

Foreword by Luke Johnson

I think the word 'work' has unfortunate connotations. For far too many people this means drudgery. By contrast, those who are able to enjoy their occupation and derive fulfillment through work are the lucky ones. For them, work is much more than earning a living – it is about finding a purpose in life, and doing something productive with their time.

I like to believe that most of us have a skill which, if used properly, is a useful contribution to society. In an ideal world we would enjoy employing that skill and it would earn us a wage. Of course things do not always work out like that. Many jobs are boring, and many of us never really discover our true metier. Others find that their real love is a pursuit which can only be practised as a hobby, for it can never generate an income.

Wise people understand themselves well, and get to know where their valuable talents lie. They exploit them to the full, but also pursue the 'Just Enough' philosophy of life. That means they do not overstretch, but rather get work and leisure in proportion. They manage to earn enough to be comfortable in their own terms, and spend quality time on other aspects of existence: family, friends, pastimes, lifelong learning, community, civic involvement and so on.

In busy modern lives, all these competing calls on one's time mean you need to be well organised and disciplined. It means you need to set priorities and use technology. While tools like mobile phones and Blackberry devices can be intrusive, they can also make you more efficient, especially in remote locations.

Few of us get the balance right all the time. There are inevitably periods where we are frantic, and other phases where we feel bored or idle. The goal is to smooth out the peaks and maintain a vital sense of engagement, without exhausting yourself or letting people down. The challenge is to remain captains of our souls.

This book should help you master that task and help you achieve a rational balance of work and play. The author has managed that, and wants to share his experience and knowledge. Good luck in your journey, and I hope Jim's words prove a useful guide.

Luke Johnson,
Chairman, Channel 4 Television and Risk Capital Partners

Introduction: The Need for Change

'We can't create change with the same level of thinking that created the problem.'
Albert Einstein

If you were hoping for an inspirational read about canine husbandry or lots of useful tips for man's best friend, you have either picked up the wrong book or should return it to whoever gave it to you. If, however, you have this in your hands to help find some answers to the critical relationship between work and the rest of your life, then you have found the right thing.

Why is Work-Life Balance Such a Big Issue Now?

Our working lives and the nature of our careers have fundamentally changed in a very short period of time. A number of forces have come together to make our working patterns more emotionally demanding and less rewarding, taking away control and having a greater impact on our whole existence. The globalisation of business and increased competition has driven companies further towards profit maximisation, usually at the expense of its staff. Many of us have been caught up in a spiraling virus of materialism fueled by the media which promotes lifestyles we cannot afford and which don't make us happier or more fulfilled. Technology has made routine tasks a lot easier but has also asked us to be accessible virtually all the time, making it difficult to switch off from work issues. Work is entering our homes and private lives far too often, changing our balance and natural working equilibrium.

Expectations have changed about when and where we are contactable and the speed at which we have to respond. We are expected to make important decisions in a fraction of the time, and we have less time to assess the direction of our career path, along with the lifestyle that will make us more satisfied and rounded as human beings. Work commitments now affect our entire lives and the people around us. The result has been losing touch with what we really want from our job or occupation and how we want to run our lives, losing track in the process of aspects of our identity. This has left many of us frustrated, unmotivated, unfulfilled and in the dark about whether we have been successful or not. Work is now affecting our state of mind and this situation is only going to get worse unless action is taken. Bringing change into our lives is therefore essential to combat the evolving nature of work and the new demands put upon us.

We spend a considerable amount of time toiling away at our desk or computer terminal, constructing plans and solving problems for other people – often making profit for unknown shareholders, directors or investors. Yet we rarely, if ever, spend time examining ourselves with the same critical eye, in an effort to understand what we want. The road to success is not always an easy or straight one and there are certainly no 'magic bullets' but by thinking differently about key aspects we can transform our approach and get back on track. It is not always about making meteoric modifications overnight but often simply by taking small steps in the right direction. Much of what follows focuses on the work part of the work–balance equation, as this is the piece of the jigsaw that usually needs attention and has been affected the most by external factors.

Content Overview

Each chapter starts with a brief statement about its aims and objectives. The whole work–life balance arena is broad and means very different things for all of us. This book therefore covers a range of topics, subject areas and viewpoints, which will hopefully provide food for thought. Personal profiles of successful businessmen and businesswomen are scattered throughout each chapter, along with quotes and ideas to provide a different perspective or light relief. The people profiled have come from just about every sector of business, from insurance to media and engineering to international education. There are individuals from a vast array of professions including accountants, marketers, solicitors, photographers, industrial designers, financiers, trainers, headhunters and pure entrepreneurs. They bring insight from different cultures and climes including France, Germany, Switzerland, Great Britain, Australia, America and Asia, drawing on commercial experience from household names such as Sony, Universal Music, Virgin, MGM, Panasonic, Cadbury Schweppes, J.P. Morgan and Diageo. Their names have been altered to protect the innocent. The reason for moving away from the classic name, job title and company is that I wanted people to feel free of their corporate ties and responsibility. I needed them to look into the fabric of their business lives and reach for answers outside their current comfort zone. Every person has one thing in common: they have reached a work–life crossroads.

How To Use This Book

A doorstop perhaps, or something to throw as catching practice for the dog? Well, you could, but it's hopefully more useful as a tool to review and alter your life. Changing the way we approach the content of our daily routines is often about making a connection with experiences or ideas outside our current comfort zone. This untainted stimulus gives us the ability to see things in a new light and break the feeling of being trapped in some kind of workplace vacuum that is sucking us dry. This book contains bites of information, stories, anecdotes, case studies and thoughts from people having similar issues to the rest of us. They all aim to slow us down enough to take a second look at what we may be missing or having to forgo. Some of these views may not apply to everyone or might even appear at times to be completely crack-pot, but the objective is to get us looking at our work and private lives from a fresh perspective.

Not all of us can, or should, walk into the boss's office tomorrow morning and hand in our resignation (no matter how tempting that might be at times) but we can find immediate satisfaction and more than a little encouragement by starting something new. There are tips from highly successful individuals on how to improve our attitude to a whole range of day-to-day issues that affect and influence our behaviour. For example, for most of us, money is vital as it makes our world go round and oils the cogs of many of the things we want to achieve. Focusing on cash alone, however, can only lead to short-term thinking, a lack of achievement and an erosion of our basic happiness. Money doesn't solve problems; having more of it often just raises the bar of expectation and usually at the expense of our lifestyle because we have to work harder to achieve it.

'Work as if you don't need the money, love as if you have never been hurt and dance as if no one's watching.' Satchel Paige

Common Themes

There have been some consistent issues coming out of the research, interviews, discussions and scouring of the commercial landscape. It is natural to imagine the problems we face relate solely to our personal circumstances but there are plenty of others out there tackling similar predicaments and the factors that are affecting our work-life balance are much the same the world over. In this book, we challenge the major issues that affect our lives:

1) Being in control – one of the most stressful situations is working in an environment where we are unable to manage things the way we would like. Someone else is pulling all the strings and conflict is often the end result.

2) Technology – considerable time has been saved performing routine tasks and our ability to communicate with others in the workplace has never been easier but there has been a considerable cost to our personal lives. For many of us work enters our homes and private space far too often and we find that technology is driving our behaviour rather than the other way around.

3) Moving target – as our careers and lives evolve, so do the things that make us happy and more fulfilled. Finding the day-to-day tasks that improve our self-esteem and confidence is a continually moving target that needs to be closely tracked.

4) Pace – our working lives are usually run at break-neck speed, giving us less time to consider the decisions we are making and whether we are going in the right direction. We need to pause for contemplation more regularly than we might imagine.

5) People – those we work with have a major influence on our state of mind and on our ability to identify what is important to us. Managing these relationships is a critical part of achieving greater harmony and equilibrium. We can all be better at it!

6) Retirement – the vast majority of entrepreneurs struggle to envisage being without some kind of mentally stimulating activity along with tasks that challenge and provide purpose. We all need to define what retirement might mean if we are to head in the right direction.

7) Timing – don't leave decisions about your career and lifestyle too late: give yourself enough runway to make a real difference.

8) Create room – if we are to make a long lasting change to our career path, we will need to clear out some of the existing precon-ceptions, activities and outdated knowledge. We have to be open to new developments and create the space to bring them into our lives.

9) Working world – our working environment is evolving at an incredible rate with a greater level of competition, customer knowledge and understanding, leading to more demands on our

time. If we stand still for very long, we will fall behind.

10) Change – anyone who thinks they have seen the tail-end of this workplace revolution, needs to hold on to their hat. The ride could get bumpy!

'There is joy in work. There is no happiness except in the realisation that we have accomplished something.' Henry Ford

Money and Success

We have been seduced into believing that money is success. That earning good salaries, having expensive cars and luxury holidays are things we must all strive for because everyone else wants them. Money is not success: balance is success. Achieving a proper, healthy, sustainable, human equilibrium must be our goal, although working out what we are really searching for is not as easy as it sounds. Almost everyone I have spoken to wants to spend less time doing the hard graft and have their workload impact less on the rest of their life, but few know how much less and what they would do with all this spare time. Some of the ideas and concepts in the following chapters are designed to provide fresh impetus and possible routes. It is only when new paths are explored, however, that we really begin to fully understand what we might want. It is not a single stage process where we turn from over-worked, half-droid to super-happy humans, it must be seen as a series of phases with regular pause for reflection. It is a progression that starts with a realisation that change is needed and thereafter a series of exciting (if nerve racking, at times) steps into the unknown.

Some Personal Perspectives

I've been very lucky throughout my working life – right place at the right time, several good breaks and even a few laughs along the way. Perhaps the most fortuitous aspect has been having people around me who have put up with my style of doing things. For me, working has never been about just performing a small mountain of tasks in a preset manner (which is probably just as well because I really wasn't very good at it), it has always been about how things are done. Personalising actions and activities has always been important, as these things were a big part of my behavioural make-up. Work has to be a very personal reflection of who I am and not just some passing comment about the sort of company, task, role or position I find myself in. The trade-off was not about money versus time at work, it was about how I did things versus time at work. I required more flexibility in the working environment to get the best results and wanted to be judged on that basis and not by how early I arrived at my desk. The key here is to identify what we are prepared to trade and what essentials need to remain on our priority list at all times.

Building business relationships has always been a much under-valued asset and we often only find out how much intellectual wealth has built up when things go wrong or we need help. Creating trust, empathy and respect can take years and may involve more than a good lunch, passing on some information or signing a piece of paper. The secret is making a special connection with people, which is often as valuable as some of the more tangible assets on your personal balance sheet or, indeed, the company's.

Some jobs look great on paper but when we get into them, there is so much politics, bureaucracy or just basic negativity that it's virtually impossible to do anything meaningful in a way that is personal. That's just not fun or productive. After all, Scheweitzer was right, 'success is not the key to happiness… happiness is the key to success'. Some of the wealthiest people I know are amongst the most discontented and unfulfilled, still searching for something that makes them whole. Most were expecting money to be that magic panacea but when they arrived at that station, it wasn't what it was supposed to be.

Pure Balance

A good friend had a profitable, fast-growing construction company and managed to turn it into a small and focused firm over two to three years. After plenty of thinking and soul-searching he realigned his lifestyle after changing his priorities. He came to understand that taking his daughter to school each morning and spending plenty of time with his family was as important as his business goals. He enjoyed work and the purpose it provided but didn't like the impact on everything else that was important to him. He felt that if he didn't do something about it in time, he would regret not having those family experiences. Managing to cut the size of his operation, while maintaining a good standard of living *and* having rice crispies with his daughter every morning, is what I call success!

Work–Life Conflict

The personal profiles in the following chapters are based on interviews with successful individuals. They have been interviewed at length about aspects of their working life and everyone has been asked about their criteria for success and achievement, what impacts on their own work–life balance, what retirement might mean and what advice they might have for the rest of us. I was fortunate enough to be able to pose the question of work–life balance to an American association called 'World President's Organisation' (WPO) which is a group imade up of people who have all been CEOs or Presidents of a company with a minimum turnover and who have worked their way to that position. Here is a summary of their responses:

* My balance comes from my career, spouse and children which provide me a series of 'reservoirs of trust'. I draw from each of these reservoirs as I need to re-balance.
* I am in balance when I am making decisions compared to those times when others are making decisions for me.
* To be in balance, I can't let someone else influence me to much.
* Being in balance means setting boundaries for myself.
* Being balanced means being a happy person with a sense of fulfillment but not to the detriment of others.
* Balance means getting up in the morning with a purpose, which includes concern for health and making a contribution to others.
* Balance for me has been a moving target, changing with age and place.
* In earlier life, I always tried to emulate someone else that I looked up to. I don't do that any more and am much more satisfied with myself.

Corporate Behaviour

When I started work back in the capitalist dark ages of the late 1980s, life seemed so straightforward. It was about how much profit we, our team, our department, our division or our company could make. Nothing else mattered. Being successful usually meant putting the rest of our life into some kind of holding pattern; working all the hours God sent; being eternally grateful to the bosses or clients; and above all, not rocking the boat. I began to see mini-clones popping up all over the corporate landscape, not just a few but virtually everywhere. All singing the company song, doing business like the top dog and thinking they were adding great value by going down the same path as their predecessors. We were being sucked into a corporate behavioural hole that removed part of our own identity, creativity and individuality. I thought this was what achievement was all about but for those of us who managed to step-off, there was a dawning of self-awareness. It reminded me of Aristotle's famous statement, 'happiness belongs to the self-sufficient'. We have become too dependent on corporate structures and trusted processes, making us a little more efficient over time but hugely reliant. It is also crushing many creative abilities and removing our confidence to try new things. The corporate culture is making us better at a few things and poorer at so many others. This trend has reached a dangerous level as companies and many individuals have lost the ability to think independently and no longer look for opportunities outside their comfort zone. The very nature of entrepreneurship is being eroded along with the appetite for individualism. The 21st-century entrepreneur must now weigh-up business success with lifestyle and see balance as a key component.

How Can We Change?

We all need to find a trigger or create a mechanism where we can find time to think proactively about our working lives and what is important. The irony is that the more so-called workplace 'success' we have, often the busier our days become and the less time there is for conscious thought. One guy I met ensures he spends one lunch time every week exploring something different. Sometimes it is just surfing the net to find sites he hasn't had time to look at; sometimes it is reading a new magazine in search of inspiration. He tries to search for inspiration outside his company, beyond his usual circle of friends and where others around him are not looking. It provides a fresh perspective on a surprisingly large number of business-related issues and his career has benefited as a consequence.

The Only Constant
If we truly aspire to obtain more from our career and the rest of our lives as well, then we have to embrace one simple concept: there is a need to change because everything around us is evolving. It won't always be easy to adopt a different position or immediately see the rewards, but to not act will be worse. I am minded of the JFK quote: 'Change is the law of life. And those who look only to the past or present are certain to miss the future.'

1 Why Do We Over-Work and Under-Play?

Aim

Changes in our working patterns, corporate culture and a host of related business forces have given rise to the endemic over-work affliction. Our behaviour at work and what we now consider to be normal are very different from a generation ago. We need to understand the impact on our mindset if we are to be prepared to fight for what we want.

We hear it again and again: 'It's not that I hate my job but I am working far too long, don't feel in control and am not achieving what I want from life.' The notion of having enough quality time with friends and family, reading a book, taking it easy in front of a good film, etc. seems to be a dream that doesn't get any closer for many as the demands of 21st-century working become ever greater. There was a train of thought that expected this trend to only affect senior managers and business owners but it is increasingly a strain on all of us. Like some kind of virus or plague, the over-work and under-play culture has slowly taken hold of our lives.

Careers often bring a strong sense of fulfillment, usefulness and stimulation to our being and behaviour. They can enrich and provide the kind of exciting mental reward that is difficult to match in other aspects of our lives. The environment in which we work, however, and the continually growing challenges can, and do, have profound side-effects. Virtually all of us lead a better lifestyle than a generation ago and everything we hear about technology is that it should make tasks easier, leaving more room for the good stuff. It's true that we hardly have to lift a finger and messages can be sent to numerous work colleagues all over the world along with detailed instructions, advice and comments. The whole idea of performing the same set of work-related tasks, however, whilst sitting on a beach with a lap-top, phone and long cooling cocktail, seems a trifle fanciful to most of us. What has happened to the dream that Marx had of thinking before lunch and fishing before supper?

C an We Be Successful and More Fulfilled?

I believe we can all be happier and influence our state of mind by changing a few simple parts of our lives. The first fundamental concept to consider is that we are rarely either totally unhappy with our lot or totally satisfied, therefore we spend most of the time somewhere moving between these two polar states. Imagine for a moment that our happiness is represented on a single line. At the right-hand end there is complete self-fulfillment and success with work and the rest of what we do. The left-hand end is where we are totally unhappy and live in a state of permanent under-achievement.

Our lives are made up of many differing elements, all of which can be plotted along this line. For me, lots of boring meetings, presentations, making decisions on subjects I am ill-equipped to make and wading through a sea of emails that have no relevance to what I do, are all situated at the left-hand end. On the right, however, sits finding new business opportunities, briefing creative projects and breaking down complicated tasks into manageable units. For many people I have spoken to and interviewed, commuting to and from work is often on the negative side, along with being contacted out of the office, work politics and the feeling of not being in control of our work destiny. It therefore follows to be happier, all we need to do is remove or reduce one or more elements from the negative side and spend a little more time doing something that sits on the other end. It sounds straightforward because it is. If we can, over a period of time, remove more things from the left-hand side, or perhaps even get them closer to the centre where they have less impact, the happier and (usually) more successful we will become.

The second fundamental concept is that we can actually influence how happy and successful we are. This is a large part of identifying what the right work-life balance is for ourselves and many of us feel there is little chance of us changing things for the better. That we are mostly powerless to influence events, especially those relating to our working lives. In my view though, what makes us the individual we have become are our thoughts and feelings, *not* the house we live in, the car we drive or the title on our business card. If this is true, then in theory all we need to do is adopt a more positive frame of mind and to think in a different way about opportunities and problems. This will transform our mindset and we will start to feel more confident, content and fulfilled. We can convert our basic outlook from cup half-empty, and alter our personality in the process. The starting point rests solely with ourselves as we have the ability in our hands to change and evolve in relation to circumstances around us.

Divided Lives

Divided Lives
I have met many people over the years who try to divide their lives into two distinct and unrelated parts: the work bit and the family/fun time. In reality, every part of our life is intertwined – how many of us haven't worked the occasional weekend, moved meetings around to fit in some social activity on a Friday afternoon, or worked flexi-time in order to be able to pick up the kids? Our working existence and the energy it saps has a huge and constant impact on our whole life and all those who are important to us. As a strategy for dealing with these two supposedly distinct parts, many people have developed two utterly different personalities. It is as if putting on the work

Personal Profile – Scott

Background – having served a ten-year apprenticeship with two firms in the insurance sector and at only 30 years of age, Scott took the bold step of starting his own company. He now employs over 120 people, operates from six separate locations and has ambitious plans to double in size over ten years. The business has developed through a mix of acquisition along with organic growth and the future is likely to be the same. He spends a lot of time developing business relationships, several of which have resulted in him buying the people and assets. Scott sees great value in knowing people well before getting into bed with them on any commercial level.

Success – to separate his personal life from his work is not always easy, as they are so closely linked. Everything he does is a reflection of his ambitious desire to do things better and part of the success equation is employing people who have determination, honesty, integrity and who take responsibility. Scott feels it's vital to work on things that he and the people around him find challenging in order to keep everyone thinking and active. Repetition just leads to a shut-down in looking at new ideas and solving problems.

Work Balance – technology is a self-confessed weakness so he employees people who have good skills in that department and looks for those who react to technology in a natural way. One of the benefits of not getting caught up in too

clothes in the morning completely masks the real person within and some kind of seriously watered-down version jumps into the car or commuter train. That is pretty sad, especially given the amount of time we now spend at work.

Cultural Shift

Our history teachers told us that during the industrial revolution, we moved from a nation of farmers and traders to one of factory-, office-, mill- and mine-workers. The hours that we worked increased and the demand for new goods and services grew exponentially on a global basis. The very nature of work and its impact on our behaviour has fundamentally much modern technology is the ease with which he can control his schedule and the priorities he wants to focus on. His PA is able to screen 80% of incoming messages, allowing him to be more proactive, rather than simply reacting to issues. He is able to have more personal time than many others in his position because his company has a strong pyramid structure. He only has two direct reports plus his PA, allowing him time to digest issues that arise rather than simply follow a well-trod path. He couldn't have the life he wants without being able to delegate effectively.

Retirement – the big exit is likely to be when he sells the business, although frankly admitting, he would then get involved in other commercial ventures as a non-executive director, investor or advisor. He believes activity, both mental and physical, is essential for enjoyment of life.

Advice – Scott says that 'running and owning your own business is fantastic. If you see things positively, then challenges are not stressful. It's also important to be quite self-sufficient, take responsibility and be mentally strong'. He also feels we need to trust people and enjoy giving that trust; getting cynical is a sure way to make things more difficult for everyone. If we form a relationship with someone in business, chemistry is the most important factor. In the same way, if we are looking to expand, diversify or acquire a company, look at the people first and the figures second.

changed. We have moved from a period where many families revolved around a single breadwinner to having both adults employed. This has resulted in the amount of time we can dedicate to family life and partners falling. Our relationships have changed and are evolving into a very different beast; by necessity there is less emotional attachment and interdependence. An increasingly mobile population has meant that friends, families and partners can be seen as almost transitional or just part of one particular phase of life. Much of this is far from being a conscious set of acts but a result of a number of social and career pressures that have come together at the same time.

Is There Any Hope For Us?

A good friend of mine recently rejected a big new job offer because of the added strain he felt it would put on his relationship and this is just one issue we now must take into account in our decion-making. The whole green and environmental revolution is, at its core, about contemplating the impact of our actions on everything around us. If we can reconnect with our true selves and place greater value on things around us that will make us happy, there may be some hope, even in the emotional deserts of large international corporations. In the book *Willing Slaves*, Madeleine Bunting outlines that nearly half of those working in Britain feel exhausted at the end of the working day. A worrying statistic! This is certainly a function of longer hours and the impact of 24/7 communication systems but also indicative of the balance between input and emotional reward.

I was chatting recently to a very successful (well, monetarily successful) guy and put a couple of questions to him about whether the second half of his working life would be the same as his first (i.e. long working days, lots of airline food, a string of problematic relationships, being close to burn-out most of the time and little awareness of anything else around him other than work). The response was very telling as he had trouble seeing past the monetary rewards and existing lifestyle; it was as if the blinkers were firmly on or a fog had descended. He really wanted his forties and beyond to be different but didn't have the first idea what the next step should be and was nervous of change. I told him to start a herb garden, take a sabbatical and do something new like learning to cook in Tuscany. Breaking

'Being responsible sometimes means pissing people off. General Colin Powell, ex-American Joint Chiefs of Staff

out of the mindset was never going to be easy for this guy as success had firmly rooted some behavioural traits that would not allow him to take the step into the life he actually wanted to be part of.

Job Satisfaction

There are lots of studies and reports into the over-work culture and the vast majority tell the same story. There are suggestions that only half of workers regularly take their full holiday entitlement every year, lunch breaks are on average down to 27 minutes (Source: Mental Health Foundation) and the amount of time we work outside the office is growing at a staggering rate. These demands are the primary cause of a decline in job satisfaction and the growing feeling of a lack of fulfilment. Most employed people and virtually all self-employed people do not receive paid overtime rates for their extra work, so why do we do it? Answers vary from job security to it now being the norm, from project demands to more responsibility or authority. Whatever the reason, this alarming increase doesn't seem like it will move into reverse without a major shift in attitude.

One of my favourite movies is Woody Allen's '*Play It Again Sam*'. One of the male characters is a very successful businessman who meets up with our star at various times, usually in restaurants and bars across New York. Upon arrival he immediately rushes over to the pay phone, calls the office and tells them how long he will be there and what the number is. The ritual becomes ever more humourous as the time spent in any one place throughout the film gets shorter and he seems to scurry faster to the phone each time. He does not actually receive any calls but always feels compelled to make sure his secretary knows where he is. Perhaps Woody Allen had a real insight into the future and the way we would become surrounded by mobile communications and computers, bleepers, buzzers and a host of other such devices, trying to ensure we don't, or can't, escape.

I had lunch with a film executive friend of mine who has climbed the corporate ladder very rapidly and now holds a position of much responsibility and status. Our hour and a half meeting usually involved him taking at least half a dozen calls and becoming completely distracted from any coherent conversation or thought process. Food is normally seen as a means to an end and something to be attacked in the same manner as most of his business dealings: with rapid pace so he can move onto the next thing. This doesn't help his almost constant indigestion and occasional ulcers. He is in his large, glass office by 8am (latest) and works through the day before spending most evenings chatting to people round the world, especially from America. He fondly remembers his early career when he still had a social life and friends he saw regularly, etc. It seemed like a long time ago to him. He has become completely addicted to the buzz and relentless activity of work.

I worked for the Hollywood film studio, Metro-Goldwyn-Mayer for a number of years and was amazed to find evening calls for UK execs were seen as the norm. It was as if anyone in Europe had to work on Los Angeles time because that's where the head office was located. I tried to shift these to emails whenever I could to provide a little more control over when and how I responded but this was usually in vain. When I confronted one American boss about this over a drink, he wasn't exactly sympathetic and thought the fact that we received more holiday than them was plenty of reward. Cheers!

Holiday entitlement is an interesting case in point. A study from Mercer Human Resources Consulting (in management-issues.com) suggests we are becoming exactly like that character from '*Play It Again Sam*'. The average number of days taken per year across Europe was 32 days (including Bank Holidays). In the UK this figure was 28 days, which compares well to America's, miserly 20 days (including National Holidays) but shows the British as a very poor relation to virtually all the main European counterparts. Figures for America are more confusing as there is a great difference in basic working relationships for many. Senior executives often have fixed term deals and many take time off between contracts. If they indeed do take significantly fewer holidays, they should perhaps open an office in Paris, then they really would have something to moan about. How we use holiday time is also important. Many sit on a beach or relax somehow rather than learning new skills or broadening our vision. Holidays are great time to put ideas and plans together. I also use them as chapter stops, assessing where I am and what path I am on.

Personal Time

What has happened to the clear lines between personal, private and work time? Everything now seems to overlap and interconnect, as we fight to establish some kind of pattern to our lives. Longer hours might be tolerable if we were able to control them to a certain degree. But don't concern yourself as help is at hand – slowdownnow.org has a ten-point beginner's guide for how to take everything in your stride.

'1. Have a cup of tea, put your feet up, and stare out of the window. Warning: don't try this while driving.

2. Spend some quality time in the bath.
3. Write down these words and place them where you can see them, 'Multi-tasking is a Moral Weakness'.
4. Try to do only one thing at a time.
5. Do not be pushed into answering a question right away. Take your time.
6. Get some zazzle.com/greencar stuff to show you're slow.
7. Yawn often.
8. Have some more tea. Tea is the drink of the slow.
9. Join our slow story reminder list.
10. Take a nap and spend at least an hour extra in bed. You deserve it.'

Perfect Working

Many of the goals and aspirations we set ourselves are now set against what I refer to as 'perfect working'. A state where everything runs on time, people are where they are supposed to be and nothing comes at us that we were not expecting. Doesn't exactly sound like my regular day! I hear so many people describe their frustration due to a delayed train, computer crashing, other people not turning up on time or the alarm not going off. Our expectations have been somehow turned, probably by a combination of advertising, technology and companies' ever-increasing search for more profit, to expect that everything is going to run like clockwork. It's as if our expectations have risen to a state that will provide us more 'free' time as long as everyone else runs perfectly. Dream on! We can only influence things within our immediate grasp and getting frustrated because things outside our control go wrong is completely counter-productive. It's not that we have lost control of our time, it's that we are trying to jam too much in! We need to build more space into our schedules to reduce expectations and the resulting tension and anxiety.

The Intensity of Work

Somehow the intensity of what we do during our working week has risen dramatically. Many of us are now asked to take charge of a more disparate set of activities and functions as well as more complicated lines of responsibility. One of the supposed advantages of the technological revolution is the ability to squeeze deadlines because we are now able to monitor the actions of others and react much more rapidly. I have a client who will always call my mobile an hour or so after she has sent an email. She expects me to reply immediately and becomes frustrated if actions aren't taken at the speed of thought. I remind her that my side of the business involves a creative process and shouldn't be rushed as the very essence of the service will be reduced. Many people I have interviewed believe they are often not taking the time to really add value to the process in the way they could.

Stop Digging

There is a notion that I've heard several times which translates to 'if we stop digging, we will die'. I guess this is trying to suggest that if we get out of this crazy rat race or remove ourselves from the information crossfire, we will somehow close down. What rubbish! All this work and life pressure has eroded our ability to understand who we really are and what makes us happy. It's natural to be apprehensive about change and the potential impact on our lifestyle and relationships. Making a connection with what makes us smile, with what gives us that lovely warm feeling (no, not the brandy!) is a proper and worthwhile goal. After all, it has taken years for us to get into this dark hole, so scrambling out is never going to be straightforward as we have dug very big craters. Even if we come to the conclusion that we need to dig in order to keep moving forward, we can at least make this a more fulfilling process by digging the holes we want to make. For example, I am much happier in my working life creating four or five smaller holes than one large one – I am able to see the fruits of my labours more readily and diversity keeps me more agile. If you are still on the fence about a move to a whole new way of working, as I was for many years, just think about some words of wisdom that a business colleague once told me. He said, 'you can't stay where you are in business, you either go up or get out. If you go up, it will mean more of the same and probably not just a little bit more. Getting out means looking at a whole new work life, away from the current occupation and/or business. Another step up the greasy pole of management will have an even greater impact on your leisure time, what things you can get up to at weekends and the idea that potentially every holiday you take will include some contact with the office. The price of success has to be measured in what we need to give up'.

Personal Profile - Derek

Background – independent, highly articulate, self-starter who has become a specialist in IT, enjoying the freedom of self-employed status for much of his working life. Derek has always been an early adopter of technology and built expertise in a particular software field that has provided a good career.

Success – many careers have natural lifecycles and the sooner we understand where we are in that process, the better we are able to deal with the inevitable changes. His particular cycle is expected to be around ten years, which is when another competitive software program is likely to bring an improved product, thereby reducing the need for his current expertise. Derek feels a measure of success in a freelance capacity is the ability to retain clients, often essential in securing a steady income flow. He has been successful for many years on this front, although he has been less active than he could be in finding new clients or exploring new commercial avenues. This is something he knows he will have to improve. One of the most rewarding elements of his job is the problem-solving aspect that he still manages to keep high on his agenda. If he is able to spend a great deal of time with clients, sorting out their system issues, then he sees that as success because it's what he actually finds very fulfilling. It is also good for his business as well.

Work Balance – when he set up on his own, there was the opportunity to put together a team to manage a large project. He had always felt insufficiently capable at managing people and also didn't really enjoy it. He likes to focus on his own performance and abilities, rather than try to improve others. He would have found spending a lot of time overseeing others much more stressful, even if monetarily rewarding. Part of his push for greater balance is ensuring technology doesn't impact on his private life too much. He doesn't like having a mobile at home and rarely thinks there is anything so important that it can't wait until the following day.

Retirement – he would like to reduce the number of days he works and start an Open University degree, probably studying something to do with history. He definitely sees any move towards retirement as being in stages, slowly phasing out traditional work and bringing in other stimulus.

Advice – the most significant piece of advice Derek has to offer is to search for a career that fits our personality before the working environment alters or adapts us. He also feels the amount of time spent watching television, playing computer games or using the net has had a profound impact on our ability to think and assess what we really want to do. There is so much information and entertainment instantly available, many of us are losing the ability to intellectualise problems and come up with the best solutions. He has always been someone who speaks his mind and although it sometimes gets him into trouble, he feels the benefits far outweigh the negatives in the long-run. People working with him always know they are getting the truth and it is rarely dressed up for anyone!

Parallel Career Paths

Our career and workplace colleagues are often inter-linked, with similar goals and objectives resulting in our performance being entwined. It took me a while to understand how my progression at a particular company could only develop at a certain pace due to the impact on others I was working with. The corporation didn't want me to stand out too much as this might de-motivate others in the team. This applied to the way I wanted to do business as well. It was exacerbated by a growing tendency on the part of my employer to evaluate everyone jointly rather than on individual merit. If you find yourself in this position, try to identify areas of responsibility and goals so that proper differentiation is possible. This will still affect some colleagues but personal achievement is as essential to our mindset as team aims. Trying to do things singularly is not an easy option, as we are often integrally linked in projects, plans, etc. in this 21st-century workspace. The lasting benefit is having a clearer vision of our own aims and objectives, leading to a career path that might be in parallel with others but separate.

> 'A real entrepreneur is somebody who has no safety net underneath them.'
> **Henry Kravis**

Cost Cutting

In their continual effort to be ever more competitive, many companies look to cut costs and often the easiest way is to restructure roles so the business can work with fewer staff. Try to recognise the signs of this happening, not just in your organisation but in those you deal with regularly. Staff cuts, slashed marketing and/or downsizing could have a significant impact on everyone! Obviously it is important to be competitive but just cutting staff will usually only result in an inferior product, service or process. Leaner periods actually offer opportunities as well as threats: grab the chance to outsource oneself or restructure deals with third parties. Most businesses I have looked at that simply cut jobs have had to do so again and again. It is rarely the answer. They are trying to improve their performance by reducing costs, not expanding their view, service, outlook or operation. Years ago I worked for The Virgin Group and many senior managers would try to break down large problems into smaller ones and give people greater ownership of their area of responsibility. This is a real art form and even when times got tough, they managed to look at combining cuts with innovative practices, thereby creating a better likelihood of business development into new areas.

Flexibility in Working, Not Just Flexible Working

In the mid 1990s a resourcing trend exploded: that of temporary work. In many sectors, short-term contractors are now seen as essential parts of the fabric. It used to be the domain of seasonal industries or those that suffered from large swings of activity but now just about every area from education to media, IT to brewing has had to embrace this move. Those sectors that have resisted this trend – banking, insurance and finance spring to mind – are certainly facing a labour shake-up. Many of us fear the insecurity of short-term contracts but they can offer more than just irregular cash. They provide a platform for exploring a whole range of other opportunities at the same time because you are not tied to one corporate mindset. I worked with a guy in the major Dutch company, Phillips, who had been there for almost 20 years. He was effectively being moved out of the organisation and decided after much soul-searching to set-up his own market research firm. He was initially very insecure about the whole process, having had a big company blanket around him for so many years. It was basically just him and the odd person he employed to do specific projects, but after a few years he managed to build a really good business. He put much of this down to having the time to explore avenues that he was never able to when he was working full time for one company. I did some work with him some years later and he couldn't conceive of returning to proper work because he enjoyed having the time to craft his trade and apply himself.

Working Harder, Not Smarter

There is a common thread of activity which runs through the vast majority of very successful people. Their inquisitive minds are continually exploring new areas of commerce and searching for improved processes. Conrad Hilton, the American businessman who founded Hilton Hotels, believes that, 'success seems to be connected to action. Successful people keep moving. They make mistakes, but they don't quit'. Exploring too many paths, ventures or ideas at the same time, however, can be hugely counter-productive. 'Success depends on getting good at saying no without feeling guilty. You cannot get ahead with your own goals if you are always saying yes to someone else's projects. You can only get ahead with your desired lifestyle if you are focused on the things that will produce that lifestyle', says Texan writer Jack Canfield, author of *Chicken Soup for the Soul*. Finding our own balance is therefore key.

Emotional Work

Apart from longer hours we are also asked to put more heart and soul into our work routines, interaction with colleagues and how we respond. It doesn't seem good enough to simply be at our desk and be supportive; we have to be waving emotional pom-poms around while we do it. This stuff also takes its toll, especially during those parts of our day that are less exciting or perhaps have a limited appeal for us as individuals. This trend towards greater emotive and expressive requirements has a direct link with self-esteem. If we are asked to put more of ourselves into something and get less from it, the risks of lower self-confidence are very real. Work-related anxiety levels are at an unprecedented level across much of the western world, even though we are wealthier and have more of what we are supposed to want. Part of this alarming trend is caused by what I call 'work attachment': we become somehow entangled in the goals and objectives of organisations and employers, making our own requirements or needs seem secondary.

One interesting solution might be what Bill Gates called his 'away days'. While at the top of the pile at Microsoft, he would go away for a few days usually twice a year on his own, with plenty of blank paper and an open mind. It allowed him to reconnect with what was important to him and look at things in a different light. The other competing influences from all sides melted into the background and it was possible to clear away some of the debris. I have suggested this to several good friends and they often respond with the fear that their partner would think they are up to no good. In a way, this *is* about separation but not from partners – from the day-to-day baggage that we are all exposed to. If two days sounds two too many then start with just one but remember that cleaning the slate takes time and can't be done in an afternoon walk in the countryside.

Real Thinking Time

Another option for getting away from the routines would be a sabbatical. This offers us the opportunity to get right away from the daily routine and see what else is out there in the farthest reaches of our thinking. Many of the top UK law firms offer a six-month paid sabbatical after a period of extended service as a partner. While I'm sure this is not solely designed for the benefit of the people involved, I can't help but see the commercial logic. Where someone has been a partner for five or six years, they have usually built up strong client relationships, are bringing on young solicitors from the junior ranks and raking in good fee income. The firm definitely doesn't want to lose them so this is a way of helping secure their emotional attachment at least until the ten-year hurdle. I have several friends who have been in this position and expected the sabbatical to trigger a major change in their lifestyles To my surprise, most opted for the *status quo* even though few of them really enjoyed their jobs. This led me to think it's either a form of institutionalisation or they go back with the intention of changing things but quickly get distracted by the importance of their position. Perhaps there is another reason: the sabbatical was needed simply to recharge the batteries and the desire to explore what else might be out there simply wasn't there.

So Why Do We Do It?

Most research and published figures seem to suggest that for the past couple of decades we have been growing increasingly unhappy at the demands that work puts on us. Are we just turning into a nation of moaners and complainers or do we have real grievances? It is certainly true that we are working longer hours and having to put more of ourselves into every day at the office. The pay cheque is certainly a factor and not just the absolute amount that arrives in our bank account each month but also the promise of more. The next rung up the ladder could be worth much more gold. This is, of course, a wondrously vicious circle as no matter how much we earn and how large our office, there is almost always the suggestion that more is tantalisingly within reach. Often these additional sums won't change our lifestyle and certainly won't improve our happiness but still we plough on in temptation.

The link between pay and overwork is all about aspiration. We aspire to have the same extension to our home as the people next door, to have a better car or all the latest gadgets and toys. Televisions are my favourite over-hyped commodity. How much better is the televisual experience on a 40-inch TV than on a 25-inch? A good friend of mine refurnished his house and now has a huge television system, which projects a picture about 10 feet across onto a whole wall. Does this really improve the experience or is this more about having a bigger one than everyone else? Oh, I forgot the 7.1 surround sound as well – I mean, how could any self-respecting, upwardly mobile guy not have it? I also asked my friend where, in this amazingly furnished abode did he think rather than just absorb or react. I'm not sure this was factored into the plans. We want smart things

> 'To be successful, you have to be able to relate to people; they have to be satisfied with your personality to be able to do business with you and to build a relationship with mutual trust'. George Ross, famed for his involvement with the American version of the popular TV series, *The Apprentice*

because we have worked so hard and therefore deserve to be rewarded. If we were able to be happy with our lot and arrive at a standard of living that is happiness-driven rather than materi-ally-driven, then perhaps the notion of having to have more money in the bank starts to look different.

'The successful manager requires characteristics such as self-awareness, self-control and the capacity for deep listen-ing, the flexibility to be both decisive and receptive to new ideas'.

Work is central to most of us and many should not want to lose the positives. A close friend of the family has run his own series of companies for many years and describes his work as

Daniel Goleman in his book, *Working with Emotional Intelligence*

a 'great train-set'. He loves working with people he likes, doing the job he loves and setting his own agenda most of the time. You might call him a very lucky guy, but not much of it has been achieved through luck alone. He knew what he wanted to achieve from his working life and, although it took many years, he has realised his goal. He also has an amazing ability to be able to switch off completely for an hour or two and not worry about the next meeting or what might be about to land in his inbox. This enables him to stay fresh. He believes happiness arrives when we are truly content with the decisions we have made.

Personal Profile - Karen

Background – born in France, Karen came to the UK to work in the entertainment business in her twenties and hasn't left. She became disillusioned with the corporate life and set up a high-end Internet home accessories company with her sister. It has been a difficult ride, especially with a small child but one that has been incredibly rewarding for all concerned.

Success – understanding what contributed to success did not come easy when she worked for large companies in the film and music worlds. Self-fulfillment on an individual level was very much intertwined with the success of her team, the division and ultimately, the company she was working for. When she started her own business, it was much easier to define what personal success would mean and for the first couple of years it was about keeping the operation trading. Since then, it has been much more about creating something that she is really proud of. Even though she had worked in big business, she didn't have a great deal of experience of dealing with people at all levels and one of the most significant achievements for her has been gaining those skills.

Ultimately success can be easily measured for her company by the level of sales in any month but for herself it is about lifestyle, first and foremost.

Work Balance – one of the most challenging things about starting out from scratch was knowing when to ask for help. Karen is very resourceful and independent and it didn't feel natural to hand over elements of the business for others to fix. IT was such an issue as she had muddled through for a couple of years, often with help from friends, but it got to a point where she needed a professional. This meant higher bills but it became easier to do the things she needed to do to keep the business moving forward more swiftly. She found the early years of her new business emotionally demanding and she had to learn how to be positive and cope with the negative feelings, especially anger and fear of failure. She believes the whole experience has made her a much better businesswoman and person.

Retirement – Karen certainly feels that the idea of retirement is yet to be worked out. She needs to put her energies into building the business and only after that will she let herself think about what the next chapter might hold.

Advice – if anyone is thinking of starting a business themselves, Karen's advice is to identify the key tasks and become skilled at them yourself. The challenge of a small business is often learning to tackle a whole bunch of activities rather than be very proficient at one specific competence. It is multi-tasking in the extreme! It is important to get into the frame of mind where we reward ourselves for handling new issues, not just doing tasks we are good at. Anyone starting out should try to keep costs very low so that all avenues are kept open. If costs do grow, it can easily have a detrimental impact on lifestyle as well as state of mind.

The Rise of the Corporation

We are perhaps at a zeitgeist turning point where many hugely powerful global businesses, often wielding more influence over our lives than governments, are making decisions that are not based solely on profit. We are moving into an era where greater value is being placed on products and services that are sourced locally and where many of us are beginning to see the benefits to our immediate environment and the world as a whole.

Joel Bakan's book, *The Corporation,* has some interesting insights, 'The corporation's legally defined mandate is to pursue, relentlessly and without exception, its own self-interest, regardless of the harmful consequences it might cause to others. As a result, I argue, the corporation is a pathological institution, a dangerous possessor of the great power it wields over people and societies'. He also goes on to say, 'Corporations now govern society, perhaps more than governments themselves do; yet ironically, it is their power, much of which they have gained through economic globalisation, that makes them vulnerable. As is true of any ruling institution, the corporation now attracts mistrust, fear, and demands for accountability from an increasingly anxious public. As a psychopathic creature, the corporation can neither recognise nor act upon moral reasons to refrain from harming others. Nothing in its legal makeup limits what it can do to others in pursuit of its selfish ends, and it is compelled to cause harm when the benefits of doing so outweigh the costs'.

If history has taught us anything, it is that every great and conquering power has been brought to its knees; been reduced to humility. Corporations have reduced the price of our lifestyle but in doing so have prioritised the consumer way of living over self-sufficiency and restraint. Like the economic revolution in 18th-century Britain and many other parts of the world since, the people caught in the wrong place at the wrong time, get the 'opportunity' to participate, all in the name of progress. Many of us are drawn into this consumerisation process subconsciously and in small steps. As consumers, however, we can all make a difference simply by looking at what we buy and consume. It is perhaps this ultimate capitalist-style democratic process that will be downfall of corporation power.

Final Thoughts - Let's Work and Play

To conclude, peer group pressure, working relationships, corporate cultures and tremendous technological changes have all pushed us towards more work and less play. This situation isn't going to magically change or go into reverse on its own, so we need to take back control of our lives. Whilst work fulfils many of our basic needs, financial being high on that list, it should not stand in the way of greater happiness. If we are able to identify what we need from our working lives, we will be able to implement change more readily. Here are some key points from this chapter:

– Work is becoming more intensive so we need to build in quality thinking time to be able to focus on what we want. This might be improved by some kind of sabbatical or 'away days'.

– Examine closely the culture of your workplace to see if it matches how you would like it to be. If the two are very different, start making changes if you can.

– Build into your schedule enough slack to incorporate things that go wrong and unexpected events. If there is too much in your working life, cut some of it.

– We need to think about how to swim against the tide.

– If we can change just one of our work habits, others are likely to follow.

– Building greater flexibility into our job is essential for greater fulfillment and personal harmony.

– Any step towards being judged, or judging others by results rather than length of time in the office will create a more positive place to work.

Random Mind Matter

* Results Matter – in a 'results-only' company or department, employees can do whatever they want, whenever they want, as long as their business objectives are achieved. Fewer pointless meetings, less stress from racing to get in at 9a.m. and no begging for permission to attend a school sports day. You make the decisions about what you do and where you do it, every minute of every

day. Cali Ressler and Jody Thompson explain more about this way of working in their book, *Why Work Sucks and How to Fix It*, or you can read more on caliandjodi.com/book. In my experience, any move towards a 'results-only' environment is a positive step in the right direction.

* Continual Contact – have we become obsessed with keeping in touch with people at all levels within our workplace? Has the fear of missing something, or being left behind in some way, got the better of us?

* Are you a 'Work Monkey' being told to run this way one minute, the other way the next? If so, it's time to show the organ-grinder you know which way to go.

* Checking-out – I had a meeting a while back with a guy who had come over from mainland Europe and who was staying in a nearby hotel. He arrived at the meeting about ten minutes late looking a bit flustered. He was usually very prompt but had tried to check out of his hotel only to be confronted by a huge queue, which hadn't put him in a good frame of mind. It is a small thing but illustrates well how we can benefit from making small changes in our lives. Hotels want us to exit in the morning so they can make sure all their paperwork is in place. I usually check out the evening before because that's exactly when others aren't standing in line and it means I have one less variable to worry about come the morning. Hotels have our credit card details if there is an extra cost, they will just put it through separately. Most of the time it just means we can plan our departure with more certainty.

* Good Times and Bad – in a blog by Lisa Cullen (workinprogress.blogs.time.com) she states the following, 'Now is probably not the time to saunter into your boss's office and demand a flexible work arrangement involving telecommuting or job-sharing or scaling back to part-time. Or is it? I've been getting and making a lot of calls from colleagues since my company announced layoffs this month. One thing I learned from an off-the-record source is that some of our magazine titles want people to go part-time. But they aren't explicitly offering part-time jobs, mainly because they hope workers who might want a part-time option will volunteer to leave altogether. So that got me to think that maybe now is the time to try to gear up some sort of non-traditional work arrangement. It's contrarian, I know. But maybe a massive economic upheaval is indeed the time for a workplace revolution'.

Sabbatical

It may just result in the life-changing experience you are looking for:

* Duration – minimum of three months and ideally longer.

* Constructive – write something, start something new, improve an important part of your life suvh as learn to create websites or rebuild a house. Make sure you do something productive and beneficial to you.

* Scenery – get a change of scenery, perhaps in a place or places you have never been before.

* Culture – experience a different culture, something that makes you review some of the norms of your current life.

* Timing – you may be surprised at how many companies now see this as a very positive thing to do.

* Plan – make a plan but build in some time and space for the unknown bits. Don't plan it too tightly and make sure there is plenty of room to adapt to the unexpected. We are looking for new experiences and will need room for these to impact.

* Return – things should not be left open-ended with work, family or friends. Define what you want to happen on your return to have something concrete to focus on.

* Asset value – you have got to see a sabbatical as increasing the value of you as an asset.

* Funky Business – Kjell Nordström and Jonas Ridderstråle launched some alternative and at times slightly crazy ideas in their book, *Funky Business*. 'Competitive advantage comes from being different. Increasingly, difference comes from the way people think rather than what organisations make. Today, the only thing that makes capital dance is talent. In such times we cannot have business as usual – we need funky business. Technology, institutions and values are being subverted and overturned. They are the triad, the interlinked drivers of change, transforming each other and creating a global village of turbulence, tribes and fusion. We are deregulating life for ourselves

> 'He that is good with a hammer tends to think everything is a nail'.
> Abraham Maslow

and our children. Whether you like it or not, we are all con-
demned to freedom – the freedom to choose,' they say.

'When you get clear about who you are being or who you want to be, you take control of your state and get clearer about achieving the goals that are important to you'.
Louise Cullum, Life Coach

2 What is Happiness and Success Anyway?

Aim

To improve our chances of being more successful, we somehow need to understand what really makes us happy, what adds to our reserve of fulfillment, what we are striving to achieve and also what is important to us. We need to look at how people, events and the workplace influence our existence and what will move things in the right direction. We also must examine how to begin to measure personal not corporate success, individual achievement and what gives us purpose.

Balancing Act

AHow is it that we find work–life balance such a difficult thing to achieve and even to define? After many interviews, discussions, phone calls and research, I put this down to two fundamental human behavioural traits, namely attraction and perception. If we are attracted to something – a cream cake for example – we desire it and therefore go and get one. Once it is eaten, our brain receives a physiological message that tells us we are satisfied and therefore don't need another one (yet!). The key is that the cut-off device is not part of the attraction process – after a few days we are likely to still desire another cream cake. The problem with the work–life equation is that there isn't any mechanism telling our mind when to stop.

'Life is like riding a bicycle. To keep your balance you need to keep moving.'
Albert Einstein

The second issue relates to how we perceive things around us. For example, we know that sunshine feels pleasant and warming but too much is not good for us. But how much is too much and when should we stop basking in the garden? In many areas of our working life, trying to create a scale for when enough is enough is extremely difficult. No bell rings in our head to say it's time we should leave the office because another late night will have a negative impact on other aspects of our life. This means we can quite easily perceive that work isn't having a seriously negative impact on us, until something major happens. I'm sure we have all seen marriages split up, people suffering from anxiety, stress, and other health issues that have made those unfortunates finally reassess their priorities, but often far too late. Somehow we need to get to that point before the calamity happens.

Moving Target

MAnother feature of work–life balance is its continually moving quality. At times, many of us feel closer to having some kind of equilibrium only to see it move further from our grasp as we get drawn by new career opportunities, monetary rewards, new toys or our personal relationships. It is undeniable that what might be almost perfect balance to some people might seem crazy and extreme to others. It is also true that we all go through a number of phases in our life and our need for job security, mental stimulation, fulfillment, personal reassurance, encouragement and people interaction can be very different in each. The traditional work–life stages are as follows:

1) Education.
2) Work hard and get ahead.
3) Work less hard because we can use our experience.
4) Put feet up.

There is an argument for saying this model is now no longer valid for a growing proportion of us as our working lives have become more complicated, diverse and fragmented. We are likely to have complete career changes, relocations, more relationships and (usually) a raft of differing work opportunities. A revised approach might look like this:

1) Education – first phase.
2) Work exposure – embark upon a career path but maybe feel it isn't quite right.
3) Re-education – second phase.
4) New improved career path.
5) Get ahead and redefine what work and life means.
6) Feet up.

Patterns of Behaviour

Patterns of Behaviour
A quick exercise: list the parts of your working life when your behaviour is not a true reflection of yourself.

Those things you do at work that don't sit well with your real personal values. These could be making quick decisions without all the facts or presentating when you hate public speaking. It's not that we set out to have different lives; it just seems that, with all the activity and responsibility of work, we have developed several persona to be able to deal with the commercial tasks that fly directly at us. When spending a lot of time performing routine tasks and playing it safe at every opportunity becomes a staple of our lives, then we may have lost some of the purpose and direction of our existence. It's like playing a sport and trying not to lose; it is very different from playing to win. Self-confidence, passion and excitement are things that shouldn't come along every now and again, they should be ever-present, driving us to do the things we want to do. One of the main reasons for this dislocation of our lives is the number of choices that get thrown at us all the time. This cauldron has led us away from understanding what we really want. We often make decisions based on what other members of society might think, rather than what might actually be beneficial for us.

What is Balance?

I have been given a great deal of interesting feedback regarding what balance between work and the rest of our lives actually means and here is a passage from a successful businessman living in the USA:

'In thinking about balance in my life, I have two vivid memories. The first was a forum exercise when we drew a big circle on each of two sheets of paper. We divided the circle on the first sheet into three sections, one each representing the time we spent on work, with family and friends, and personal time. Once we felt we had the time allocations about right, we took the other sheet and divided that circle into how we would like to spend our time – work, family and friends and personal. The contrast was an eye-opener for me. My circles were divided quite differently. They put in black and white what I was feeling, which was the excessive time I was spending on business and related activities. I enjoy being with people and social activities but I also need my time. This exercise made me face the reality of what I was doing versus what would be more satisfying.'

> 'The only thing you can change in the world in yourself, and that makes all the difference in the world.' Cher

'The other vivid memory started in mass one Sunday morning. The homily was either not too exciting or I was preoccupied. Anyway, my mind was not in church, but perhaps the atmosphere led me to a more important matter that morning. I had been feeling stressed, very stressed, but had not focused on why. I took out a pen and a piece of paper and starting writing down things for which I was responsible. Some were business, some club- and civic-related while others were family-oriented, etc. By the time I finished I had 14 items on my list – the problem was obvious. I knew the direction of the 'solution'. I did not go home from church, but went directly to my office. I expanded on the sheet by adding two columns – 'exit?' and 'when?' Before I left the office, I wrote two letters of resignation, had a plan for exiting seven obligations at natural or appropriate times, and left five on the list I wanted to continue. I sure felt good driving home.'

'In thinking back, I believe the greatest hindrance to achieving balance in my life was perhaps the lack of awareness. It took me a long time to become aware or to realise why I was uncomfortable and stressed. Once I focused on this issue (perhaps it was the grace of God that Sunday), the rest was easy. I knew what to do and did it. A close second hindrance is the lack of boundaries. The more "mature" or at least comfortable I have become, the more I am conscious of the importance of establishing good boundaries. We are all asked to do or believe we should do a lot of things, especially as we appear to be more successful. I give each request a good examination of conscience, and then if appropriate I say "no". It is OK to decline.'

Personal Profile – Joseph

Background – a highly successful account manager and sales director in a number of computer and technological fields, Joseph decided it was time for a complete change of career soon after he turned 50. He recounts the old saying that few people lie on their deathbed and wish they had spent more time in the office. After a corporate restructure he found an exit route from his job but turned down similarly well-paid positions in order to retrain as an adult teacher and trainer. His change in mindset had been driven by the fear of looking back at a lifestyle opportunity not taken. The move meant he might have to be more careful with money and have fewer luxuries, but he could stay in the same house and drive the same car.

Success – Joseph enjoyed the challenge of being in big business but always felt the lifestyle had a negative impact on what he could do with his family. This was partly the result of not being at home enough but also with the way he was still distracted by work issues when he was there. It was as if his work was like a shadow and it often stopped him having proper relationships and conversations. It wasn't just about trying to work an hour less in the office, it was about freeing his mind when he wasn't in the office. The actual process of retraining and going into a new direction has been hugely beneficial and gave him the chance to reassess what was important to him. While he was working full time he did manage to develop a strategy for switching off. He would either go for a quick drink after work or a walk, clearing the mind of as many work thoughts as possible.

Work Balance – Joseph had one boss who started early and finished late; a real workaholic. This guy thought his own job was so important it needed him to be at his desk 12 hours a day in order that everyone (including himself) knew how vital the role was. It wouldn't have been so bad but his actions affected others and gradually people began to spend longer in the office. The culture of the department and team changed due to one person and not because the business needs had altered. After the new career had started, Joseph found himself with more time and used it to do a whole bunch of things, which increased his pleasure, provided more mental stimulation and sense of fulfillment. He learnt Spanish, went on a gardening design course, became captain of his golf club and other varied things.

Retirement – sees this as a period when we still need to achieve things and fulfill goals. Definitely at a slower pace, but the introduction of new things will be as important during any retirement phase as when we are working full time.

Advice – Joseph advises everyone to read Anthony Robbins, the success guru. The first step out of our current lifestyle is the hardest, everything else follows and is much easier. Finding the right thing to do is not easy so we have to keep chipping away, moving in the right direction until we stumble across it. Most of the satisfied people he has met are able to see the tangible benefits of their actions quite quickly and if work does not provide this, we should find other things in our life that do. We need to somehow find a mechanism that allows us not to let work affect our whole lives. He believes the biggest influence on our level of happiness is lack of control followed by lack of influence over the outcome of events. When many of the things that we undertake are out of our control or not fully under our own influence, we slip into stress and unhappiness. It's during these times that we need to rethink and reprioritise.

How Did We Get Here?

Our career path and many of our daily routines are far from a simple reflection of what we do best. Our tendencies and instinctive thoughts have often been over-ruled or sidelined by opportunities that present themselves. Far from being planned or logical, our careers are often just a series of chance meetings, spontaneous happenings or being in a place at a particular time. This means that the shape of our professional lives has as much to do with chance and coincidence as it does with our innate skill set or talents.

What is Success?

'If I hadn't badly damaged my knee as a teenager I would likely have been a sportsman. If I hadn't been dyslexic I wouldn't have left school at sixteen and created a magazine, which means I wouldn't have ended up running *Student*, which means Virgin Records would never have been born, which means…' Richard Branson, in his book, *Business Stripped Bare*.

I have a publishing friend who when asked about tips on reducing stress and improving happiness, sat back in his chair and said, 'To reduce stress I drink more and to improve my happiness I drink less'. Sometimes the right balance in our lives is not always easy to find.

My nephew is keen to learn and likes to discuss his future career. One day he asked me when did I know what I wanted to do? I wasn't trying to be unhelpful or deliberately confusing but replied, 'when I find out, you will be the first to know'. I always knew that I wanted to be successful and felt the only way to find out which direction was best, was to set off and see what came along. It was not the most sophisticated plan, and as advice goes wasn't that helpful, but it was true! Many people I speak to today look at opportunities, job descriptions or career turning points and feel they are not right or don't sound exciting enough. Let's face it – most jobs don't. I'm sure if I tried to define most of the things I have done, they might not appear that fantastic either but I have enjoyed every phase without exception. Each step has provided a platform to learn and interact with many good and talented people. This is a rather long-winded way of saying that we all have a large number of avenues to explore and probably need to take a good look before we can really say they are not for us. The key for me was never to sit still and rest for very long!

Path of Discovery

Exploring new opportunities, however crazy they may seem to friends or family, are keys to opening our mind and casting off conservative feelings and inhibitions. Just about every entrepreneur I have ever met has the ability to look at things differently and see opportunities all over the place, at times driving those closest to them mad. It's not everyones cup of tea but it is one of the defining attributes of really good, multi-disciplined, multi-talented business people to be able to search for gold where others stop at the outer gates.

A True Story

This guy was selling motor trucks for a living in New York thought he was just about as unhappy as he could get. He despised his job, could only afford a small, lonely flat full of cockroaches, saw little opportunity for advancement and longed for a better life. He had studied at the State Teachers College at Warrensburg, Missouri and needed to find the courage to change. The only thing he could find was an evening class teaching adults who were paying for lessons that helped them in business. They needed to develop self-confidence, to be motivated to do things differently and help solve the key problems they faced on a day-to-day basis. Anyone who has spent any time in New York knows that these people, who were paying for tuition out of their own pocket, were likely to be a tough audience and not suffer fools for one minute. This guy loved the challenge and the success of the course soon grew, along with the scope of the material covered. The course was one of the first of its kind anywhere in the world and soon became known internationally. It evolved quickly into *How to Win Friends and Influence People*, and led to the bestselling book of the same name. This is the true story of Dale Carnegie.

Personal Profile – Nicolas

Background – an accountant and budding entrepreneur, creative thinker and someone who appreciates the finer things of life. Although only in his early thirties, he is exploring a second career based on a good online concept and is always looking at ways to increase his commercial knowledge.

Success – Nicolas believes there are three very different forms of success. First, there's conventional success, such as achieving a professional position that is traditionally well respected. This type is defined by society and we have succeeded when we reach a position that other people associate with respect, status and knowledge. This type usually brings financial rewards and the trappings of the lifestyle such as a big car, expensive clothes and a large house. Second, there is personal success, defined by the achievement of personal goals, but these are often set by others rather than ourself. These goals are seen as the reason we strive to achieve and make progress in life, and they give us the direction we need. Third, is unexpected success, often resulting from making the wrong decisions or failing to do things. When we participate in unplanned activity and/or find ourselves in unexpected places, we discover new talents, skills, opportunities and aptitudes. This brings rich rewards as others around us may expect us to fail, when actually we turn things into a success.

Work Balance – the notion of working too hard and too long either implies working is a negative activity or the extra energy and time spent could be directed towards other things. We should disregard the amount of time we spend at work; regardless of actual hours spent there if someone dislikes their job, they will feel they are working too hard. A friend of Nicolas is an antique dealer and this was always something he wanted to do. He is self-employed and there are few days when he does not work or think about business issues. However, because his work is his passion, he does not feel he works too hard and is totally rewarded by his working life.

Retirement – this means leaving the employ of others and becoming the boss.

Advice – we need to be aware that technology can be a big help but also a hindrance. Nicolas found getting a

BlackBerry® wasn't for him as it meant he kept prioritising work over his personal life, mainly because he would inevitably respond to colleagues straight away. He also believes it is important for all of us to distinguish between what is important and what is urgent. They are rarely the same.

Get Out The Tape Measure

Money is considered by many to be the first and often the only measure of success. It's certainly an easy indicator and a benchmark by which we can compare how we are getting on against others around us. However, it is an unsophisticated yardstick and offers only the simplest of indicators. Cash is certainly important as it enables us to do things and, to a certain extent, be the masters of our own destiny. But many of the most unfulfilled and confused people I have ever met have been in the wealthy category. Money therefore cannot be the only gauge and what we actually do with our cash – however much we have is often a far better indicator of how happy and successful we might be.

Most of the times I have felt successful in my life have corresponded to when I have been busy and my mind has been fully engaged with a variety of interesting and challenging tasks. It's as if I feel most fulfilledl when I have real purpose and can tick things off a list, rather than necessarily those times I am working on are the, most important and pressing things to do. This is a trait that several of my bosses over the years have commented upon and which even today, still occupies my thinking. I'm never sure if this makes me outwardly more or less successful but inwardly it definitely adds to the happiness levels. I have a great admiration for people who talk fondly about creating things they are truly proud of and if they happen to make some money along the way, then that is the icing on the cake. I have certainly tried to get the right things on the list and not just put things on there so I can have the pleasure of crossing them off.

Why Do We Worry?

The other way to look at happiness is from the opposite end. If we don't worry, then things have surely got to be OK, haven't they? Worry, deep concern, anxiety, angst, unease, fear and so on can grow within all of us at times. If these symptoms get to a level where they affect our outlook, mindset and decision-making, we need to take action. One way to find out if you suffer in some way is to ask a selection of trusted work colleagues. Get them to be honest and candid with you. On a scale, how much do you worry and does it affect your behaviour and decision-making? What are the circumstances that affect your behaviour the most? Even if the results are positive, monitor the situation as lady-luck can have strange habits.

I had a client for several years who was in a middle management marketing role and good at her job. Several promotional opportunities passed her by in close succession, however, and she became angry about being left behind. Given she had been in the company a lot longer than many others who were now higher up the pecking order, she felt overlooked. Her demeanour became less positive and I could tell it was affecting her management style. We came to the end of a long project and had a final meeting to round things up and she clearly wasn't happy with her lot and needed some help. I am usually quite reserved about jumping straight in without testing the water but I really felt she was a good person and very capable. I outlined that the senior management were all very get-up-and-go sorts of people and probably favoured similar types. They didn't want anyone who might defuse their energy and drive. I felt this could have contributed to her being pushed sideways. Over time she did change her outlook and did look visibly more energetic and forward-thinking. I wish I could say she got the next big promotion but before that could happen she accepted a job with another company. I did get an email saying she enjoyed working with me and thanked me for the advice that had helped in getting this new position. I told her it was always much easier looking in from the outside than the other way round.

> 'When I look back on all these worries, I remember the story of an old man who said on his deathbed that he had had a lot of trouble in his life, most of which has never happened.'
> Winston Churchill

Playing to Win

Fear of failure can easily become the perfect excuse for inactivity. I was asked to evaluate a marketing communications issue for an industrial company, met all the people concerned and discussed the scope and duration of the project. All seemed to be going well but there was a big question that needed asking. The personnel all seemed proficient and capable, so why weren't they doing this themselves? Why did they want an outsider? It certainly wasn't that I had some special insight, experience or flair that was essential to this task. I kept my lips as closed as I could during the meeting but cornered two of the senior guys after the session. It emerged the real reason for getting me involved was that no one internally wanted to take responsibility as they weren't sure this was going to succeed. The fear of being attached to something that had an uncertain future was very real. I took on the project not only because the price was agreeable but also because I wanted to be attached to projects that no-one else wanted. I liked the idea of being known as someone who didn't worry about tackling difficult, unpopular or politically sensitive topics; it enhanced what I saw as the space that I wanted to work in. I looked at this as a 'no-lose' situation in that everyone expected it to be problematic so any amount of success was an achievement.

The Worst-Case Plan

I have a four–point process for adding momentum to difficult work problems or projects that seem to have stalled:

Step 1 – identify the exact issue that needs attention.

Step 2 – evaluate the situation fully, from all sides and angles, and come up with the very worst-case scenario. This means the result from total and complete failure.

Step 3 – Accept the worst case in your own mind and believe that anything better would be a real result.

Step 4 – Get stuck in to make sure that the worst that could happen, doesn't happen.

Road Ahead

Bill Gates is clearly a very positive individual. There is a section from his book, *The Road Ahead,* which summarises his attitude. 'Just because I'm optimistic doesn't mean I don't have concerns about what is going to happen to all of us. As with all major changes, the benefits of the information society will carry costs. There will be dislocations in some business sectors that will create a need for worker retraining. The availability of virtually free communications and computing will alter the relationships of nations, and of socioeconomic groups within nations. The power and versatility of digital technology will raise new concerns about individual privacy, commercial confidentiality, and national security. There are, moreover, equity issues that will have to be addressed. The information society should serve all of its citizens, not only the technically sophisticated and economically privileged.'

Individual Success

'To what do you attribute the success you've had? When I was growing up my Mom was home. She wanted to go to work, but she waited. She was educated as a teacher. The minute my youngest sister went to school full-time, from first grade, Mom went back to work. But she balanced her life. She chose teaching which enabled her to leave at the same time we left, and come home pretty much the same time we came home. She knew how to balance. When I got married and had a child and went to work, my day was all day, all night. You lose your sense of balance. That was in the late '60s and '70s; women went to work, they went crazy. They thought the workplace was much more exciting than the home. They thought the family could wait. And you know what? The family can't wait. And women have now found that out. It all has to do with women, or the homemaker leaving the home and realising that where they've gone is not as fabulous, or as rewarding, or as fulfilling as the balance between the workplace and the home-place.' Martha Stewart

Personal Profile – Donald

Background – journalist, ex-professional sportsman, publisher, television producer, author, company director and Member of Parliament, Donald is the embodiment of the notion that we should not be afraid to try anything and push back the boundaries of what we know.

Success – success is often about learning to handle failure, making peace with our efforts and continuing to put maximum effort into everything. Donald believes we should all think about re-training and investing time in pursuit of new skills, which continually add to our self-confidence and career options. Exploiting fresh opportunities and searching for new things is as much about people as talent; it is individuals who open doors. Our work-based relationships are therefore a critical factor in our success. Donald also feels we need to look at how open we are and try continually to make sure others are aware of what we want. Getting out of a rut is often about putting a string of ideas on a washing line: some could take many years to come to fruition but a good idea is still a good idea. If it doesn't work right away it might be that the timing is not quite so we just need to keep it visible and not call it a failure. As an example, he worked on a concept of an online open day with an organisation and it took almost ten years to get off the ground. Now it has grown into a substantial annual event. Fear of failure is far too high in many people yet in America, failure is often considered close to success rather than the other end of the spectrum. It is also worth remembering that many corporations have the same fear of failure and getting a green-light is often about limiting their exposure or downside.

Work Balance – Donald has always worked hard and has, at times, struggled to find the right balance between family, friends and all the other things. He believes to get lucky, we need to focus our attentions, apply ourselves and spend plenty of time actually thinking things through. Life balance can be improved by using new technology, rather than allowing it to use us. Being web-centric in our thinking and application is absolutely crucial in maximising the potential of ideas and business as a whole.

Retirement – he believes the traditional view of putting one's feet up is not healthy. After an active life why should we suddenly come to a grinding halt? Taking our foot off the accelerator, however, and scaling back commitments, especially those in areas we don't enjoy, can be a great help. Retirement should be seen much more as a portfolio existence, with at least one day set aside for independent thinking rather than just interacting with others.

Advice – if we have an idea, we should be prepared to give away a chunk of equity or profit to get the thing going; 50% of something is always better than 100% of nothing.

What Others Will Say!

A friend came round to my house for lunch and we sat chatting in the living room for a while after a rather large helping of my fish pie. He looked at my television, which hasn't been replaced for some years and which is very modest in terms of size by today's lofty standards. He said he was expecting me to have a much larger one and I remarked that it had a good picture and was very happy with the proportions. I had no need for a huge screen mounted on the wall with speakers all over the place, so why have one? There does seem to be a growing pressure to keep up with others and far too much concern about what our friends, family and colleagues might say if we somehow lower our standards below some arbitrary level. If we do spend more time working, the most obvious way to evaluate ourselves is by comparison with what it brings us in the way of material possessions: a vicious cycle if ever there was one.

Life Without Work

I asked a bunch of business people who work very long and hard, what they would do if they didn't have their current job. Most felt I was getting at how they might react if they were made redundant and suddenly found themselves with lots of time on their hands. That wasn't exactly where I was going but deliberately kept the line of questioning open to interpretation. Most wanted to 'get out' at some point in the future but seemed remarkably reserved about when and how. Many of these professionals wouldn't need to go back into a big corporate set-up, at least on a full-time basis, but were still attracted to elements of it. In my mind, they had done the hard work and now could explore new opportunities. Most had blinkers on, however, when it came to looking at alternative ways of living and it seemed as if their 'success' at work had reduced their confidence or desire to do other things. One would think that the exact opposite would be true – that if they were good at something, they could go on and be good at other things that perhaps provide more fulfillment and flexibility. While there was a whole host of reasons for being reluctant to try new things, the fear of failure and not reaching the same high standards were definitely high on the list. Many enjoyed their influential and prestigious roles and were reserved about a job that might not provide experiences relating to self-esteem. Confidence inside their current careers was high but when I put a range of other possible professions or lifestyles, most seemed to see the downsides first, rather than the opportunity to acquire new skills. Getting these people to the first step could take some time.

The Self Scale

How do you value the various aspects of your life? Where does the fulfillment, self-esteem and self-respect that we need to keep evolving as humans come from? From what I have read and found out about many businessmen and businesswomen who have been propelled into high-flying positions, the value system for many people is geared largely to their jobs and not other aspects of their life. It's as if being a good father, getting the golf handicap down to single figures or helping others less fortunate, all pale into insignificance on our own self-scale. We are increasingly assessed by others on the basis of what we do in the workplace rather than the kind of human being we are. If we were to rank ourselves on how well we were able to relax or what improvements we had made to our bodies, perhaps we would all begin to see things differently. If we were able to evaluate ourselves on how much time we have spent helping others, imparting knowledge or acquiring new skills, again the situation might look different and rosier.

One of the reasons it is vital to analyse this situation is the impact it has on our ability to gather impartial facts. Getting into a negative mindset or the desire to keep walking down the same path, is not something that happens overnight and small changes that edge in over time are often imperceptible to us. It usually takes others to offer an alternative perspective, gather useable data and present it in a useable fashion. We are too close! It is important, however, to create our own framework right at the start to properly channel the stream of data coming in. Otherwise we may become bogged-down in the assessment of what is right and wrong, when the time comes to move forward. Experience has taught me that it is important to arrive at a quick resolution. Most of the time any decision is better than none at all, moving from where we are, removing the inertia of the status quo and gaining immediate feedback on the new position are all helpful.

Sporting Business

There are some good and worthwhile parallels that can be drawn between sport and business. I have studied many sportsmen and sportswomen and believe differences in performance at all levels can often be brought back to something that goes wrong. Better performers are those who are able to block out the negative aspects of 'why did I do that?' or 'what a lousy shot, how could I have been that bad?' and calmly assess why performance was less than their best and how they think they can remedy that next time round. Good players will then walk in and play the right shot (i.e. not be reactive, overly bold or rash) while poorer players will often try to make amends for their earlier actions. We can't affect what we have done but we can make the best of the position we find ourselves in whether it be in business or on a sports field. Often the key to this is not letting our past experience and negative emotions influence the current decision we face. If we can appreciate that we will make mistakes from time to time, our response is usually better.

De minimis non curat lex – the law does not concern itself with trifling things. And neither should we! It's easy to get distracted and worried about the small things, life is far too short for that. If we are going to worry, we should do so about the big things!!!

Searching for Answers

The work of the British philosopher, Bertrand Russell has always intrigued me and this passage from *Portraits from Memory*, gives great insight into a man who worried and searched for answers all his life. 'I wanted certainty in the kind of way in which people want religious faith. I thought that certainty is more likely to be found in mathematics than elsewhere. But I discovered that many mathematical demonstrations, which my teachers wanted me to accept, were full of fallacies... I was continually reminded of the fable about the elephant and the tortoise. Having constructed an elephant upon which the mathematical world could rest, I found the elephant tottering, and so proceeded to construct a tortoise to keep the elephant from falling. But the tortoise was no more secure than the elephant, and after some twenty years of arduous toil, I came to the conclusion that there was nothing more that I could do in the way of making mathematical knowledge indubitable.'

'It is an amazing irony of life that as soon as we admit publicly that we have made a mistake, we immediately feel smarter and in the eyes of many people we are, in fact, smarter.' Anonymous

Confidence
I read an article in a newspaper about the well-known and very successful designer, Karen Millen. She started her UK fashion business at the age of just 19, with £100 in her pocket. At its peak in 2004, it had 130 stores and when things got a bit tougher for her personally, she decided to sell which turned out to be a very wise move. She described the period that followed as recharging the batteries, building confidence and having plenty of 'me time'. It occurred to me that confidence can be such a fragile thing. Karen had achieved a huge amount but because that success didn't continue to go upwards, her self-assurance and self-belief, were being challenged again. Money was no longer a concern for her but she still had that need to achieve and move forward in the pursuit of goals that were important to her. Like many of us, the route to happiness in this phase of her life isn't about looking back at what she had done; that wouldn't help a bit.

It's about setting new aims for this energetic and lively person, ensuring she still has mountains to climb.

Final Thoughts – Just Do It!

There is a strong argument that we really only learn by actually doing tasks and getting first-hand experience. Happiness and success are never easy to fully identify without that understanding. Our ambitions and aims also change over time providing us with constantly moving goalposts about what is important to ourselves and the people around us. Here are some key points from this chapter:

– We need to regularly measure success against our own goals not the aims of others.

– Money is only one of the ways of measuring success and is a very simplistic yardstick.

– Simplifying projects, tasks, relationships and our career decisions is a success in itself.

– Our working environment has led us away from feelings of security and self-awareness to corporate desires and profit objectives.

– Share key decisions with trusted, selected people. Bring other perspectives into our world.

– If you were without your current job, what other avenues would you explore? It's a very useful exercise to starting looking at these paths.

– Many of us don't really know what career we want to do and what makes us truly fulfilled, it's only by trying different things and keeping a very open mind, that we can achieve a better understanding.

> 'The room for a conscious effort towards happiness is to be found in the pressure-opportunity gap.'
> **Edward De Bono**

Random Mind Matter

* Michael Breen, the international NLP practitioner had this to say when asked about work-life balance: 'Does [a poor life balance] mean that one hasn't sorted out priorities and crafted one's life accordingly? Are we really talking about the stress from over-commitment? Happiness is always available to us but, in modern times, we have reframed and misdirected the word to signify exuberant joy.

Happiness is the sense of open, simple presence, where ordinary living circumstances are neither perceived as threats to life and limb or prizes and rewards. Happiness is an intense feeling of being alive and vibrant with it. We live in an extraordinary era where we have more choices for how we pursue our lives (and their inherent obligations and commitments) than at any other point in history. Television and the media, cultural norms and modern life leave most of us in a state of perpetual desire without the ability to satisfy those desires – perpetual hunger, perpetually in a state of 'where's mine?' and 'what about me?'.'

* If the Right Size Fits – in 1996 Tamara Mellon approached East-End shoe couturier Jimmy Choo, with the idea of joining forces to launch a brand new shoe company. She put together investors, agreed deals with manufacturers and set about establishing the business. She opened the first shop in London the following year and established a highly lucrative wholesale business to other retailers as well. The essence of her vision was the brand must always be seen as stylish and upmarket, a touch of the exclusive. The creative team understood that searching the world for the unusual, whether it be beading, lace or other materials and styles, can be very inspirational. Looking at things that many people saw around them didn't have enough mystique. This philosophy meant they looked different from their competitors. Their online boutique (jimmychoo.com) is always worth a look for a simple way of showing elegance.

'I've developed a new philosophy – I only dread one day at a time.' Charlie Brown

* What Got You Here - the book, *What Got You Here Won't Get You There: How successful people become even more successful*, written by Marshall Goldsmith outlines 20 habits that can hold us back. They are:

1) Winning too much.
2) Adding too much value.
3) Passing judgement.

4) Making destructive comments.

5) Starting with 'No', 'But' or 'However'.

6) Telling the world how smart you are.

7) Speaking while angry.

8) Negativity.

9) Withholding information.

10) Failing to give proper recognition.

11) Claiming credit.

12) Making excuses.

13) Clinging to the past.

14) Playing favourites.

15) Refusal to express regret.

16) Not listening.

17) Failing to express gratitude.

18) Punishing the messenger.

19) Passing the buck.

20) An excessive need to be me.

* Modern Challenge - 'The greatest challenge to organisations is the balance between continuity and change. You need both. At different times, the balance is slightly more over here, or slightly more over there, but you need both. And balance is basically the greatest task in leadership. Organizations have to have continuity, and yet if there is not enough new challenge, not enough change, they become empty bureaucracies, awfully fast.' Peter F Drucker, writer, management consultant, and self-described 'social ecologist'.

> He has achieved success
> who has lived well,
> laughed often, and loved much:
> Bessie Anderson Stanley, 1904

'The secret of being miserable is to have the leisure to bother about whether you are happy or not.'
George Bernard Shaw

* Retirement – here is a quote from one very successful businessman; 'What does retirement mean? I don't know. I am not retired so it is hard to imagine. A friend asked me last week if I was retired. I told him, no, I go to the office and work every day. The next question followed logically; what do you do? Whatever I want to, I replied. Isn't that great? I have more to do than I have time for. I am doing what I want to do because I am interested. Yes, there are some continuing obligations, but I do them by choice. As a side note, perhaps an essential for not retiring (and perhaps personal happiness – I am distinguishing this from family, love, health, etc.) is the thirst for learning. There are so many things I want to know/know more about that I cannot imagine ever getting bored, which is perhaps what retirement is.'

3 Are You Right-Brain Dominant?

Aim
In this chapter we take a detailed look at how decisions are made, what helps form our preferences, how likes and dislikes affect our workplace behaviour and what kind of businessperson we really want to be. Working well with others is an essential skill and something where little real training exists to help us improve. A major part of being successful and happy in our career progression and most aspects of our life requires a growing level of self-awareness and an understanding of how we are perceived by others.

'You can never plan the future by the past.'
Edmund Burke

'Genius does what it must, and talent does what it can' Owen Meredith

Expressive Understanding

Innovate or die. A commandment used by many technology companies over the last decade or two in response to the ever-growing competition in this area and now a phrase that actively dictates the pace of our working lives. Computers, software programs and the net have enabled us to transform not just the way we do business, but the very essence of what skills and aptitudes we need to succeed. For many of us, along with companies of all shapes and sizes, the equation is not simply whether to evolve but how fast we need to adapt? Evolution is much easier to say than do, and achieving a state where ideas, perceptions and processes collide positively to create change, can be unnerving for just about everyone involved. For example, change can create disputes and differences can become personal. If this happens, the creative process can break down or go into reverse, before it has a real chance of success. Understanding how we think, along with how we are perceived by others, are key steps to unlocking creativity, making a difference in the workplace and experimenting with new ideas.

Knowing Me, Knowing You

Part of our ability to adapt and innovate depends on how well we know ourselves: our strengths, weaknesses, likes and dislikes. We all have natural preferences and many successful people are not only highly in tune with their own personality but also have greater harmony between work and life activities. Having an in-depth understanding of our own behaviour and reactive traits can improve our communication skills, help us resolve conflict, read people's reactions and work with others more effectively. We are all different but it is possible to categorise our reactions and improve our response to others in key situations. The vast majority of our decision-making is far from random; it is the result of our preferences, subconscious attitudes and traits, highlighting the way forward.

The most widely accepted analysis in the area of cognitive behaviour splits the brain into two parts. We are either a right-brain person or a left-brain person. It's not that all left-brain individuals have a huge vacuum on the other side but more often than not, one side is more dominant. Left-brain people usually have a sequential, analytical and logical way of approaching problems. This differs from the more intuitive, non-linear and emotional response of right-brainers. Much of the work in this area is built on Myers-Briggs Type Indicator (MBTI), a questionnaire-based research tool that was designed to measure psychological preferences. This in turn owes a great deal to the work of Carl Gustov Jung, who published *Psychological Types* in 1921.

'Whatever the circumstances of your life, the understanding of type can make your perceptions clearer, your judgments sounder, and your life closer to your heart's desire.' Isabel Briggs Myers

Information Processing

The fundamentals of this approach lie in looking at how we assimilate data, make decisions and relate to other people.

This is not a tool that ranks or appraises our various abilities, it's about preferences. For example, you may prefer to approach a particular issue using your instinct and initial emotional response. But your training might tell you to take a second look and use a more methodical process: your past experiences may have created habits and ways of dealing with certain circumstances. This is usually because those experiences are saying, it worked last time so let's give it a go again!

The professions, occupations and careers we choose are rarely down to fortune; they are affected by our own preferences. For example, we instinctively gravitate towards roles which reward what we are naturally good at or feel comfortable with. This is not always a healthy trend as we can quite easily keep marching down that same furrow, year after year, thinking it's the only way to go. This can also be a self-perpetuating process, for the longer we work, the more likely we are to be attracted to the way we have always approached issues. These instructions can be at odds with our general way of working or what we might now want to achieve.

It's Only Words

You may be surprised to know how people with different personalities interpret the words we say and our own style can stifle the creativity of those around us. Making sure we all acknowledge the existence and need for very different types is a huge step forward in building something worthwhile. Most highly successful teams rely on a range of viewpoints, opinions and input for their underlying creative energy and direction. Like an individual, if a group is heavily dominated by a left-brain mindset it is likely to be short of lateral thinking and long on analysis. In a situation like this, there's usually a lot of numbers, assessments and thorough research and not much imagination. The few right-brainers may find it difficult to get their point across and often end up agreeing with a course of action because it seems too difficult to do anything else.

> 'We all have thought processes that dominate how we make decisions and even interact with people around us.'

Our preferences can have a positive or negative impact, depending on the situation. A person who needs quiet reflection may not be great in a crisis that requires immediate and decisive action. On the other hand, a heavily analytical person can often come across as cold and ruthless, leaving people with little sense of loyalty or mutuality. Understanding other people's approach and preferences will help you communicate and collaborate, forming a healthy bond of respect and workplace understanding.

Start with Yourself

When we are able to identify our own style, it will provide tremendous insight into the way our instincts unconsciously direct decisions, actions and even the way you communicate with others. It's important to remember that we should treat people the same way we want to be treated ourselves. Some years ago a good friend of mine took me for a drink one evening after a meeting had gone spectacularly wrong. I had put forward a strong message at the session but, in hindsight, was preaching to people who thought I was too pushy, too confident and too self-assured. I had to learn that adapting the content of any message for the receiver and not just the sender was a key component of success. I had much to learn!

We can take the left-brain and right-brain analysis a stage further by splitting each side of our head into two further parts, giving us four quadrants. The key features in each quadrant are set out below – see which one most closely fits your personality. It's worth remembering this is not about what you would like to be but who you really are. It's not an exercise to find out where you may be poor but a look at your instinctive orientation. You also don't have to be all the things in a particular sector for it to be the right one. A good way of starting is to try to rank the four quadrants; one being your best and four being the worst.

Left-Brain vs Right-Brain Quadrants

Perception and Reality

One great application of this analysis is how we are perceived by different sorts of colleagues. Try to list half a dozen or so people you work closely with and see where they might sit. Place them in the quadrant that most closely suits their dominant traits. Depending on your business, function or overall working requirements, you might see a bias to one side or another. For example, we would expect most accountancy firms to be strongly represented in the A and B categories. A marketing consultancy, however, might have lots of Ds with a few Cs thrown in for good measure.

The exercise gets more interesting when looking at how we might be perceived, either as individuals or in groups, or even whole companies. Here is how you are often thought of by others in the diametrically opposing quadrant:

> 'We can hear exactly the same message from two people and interpret it completely differently.'

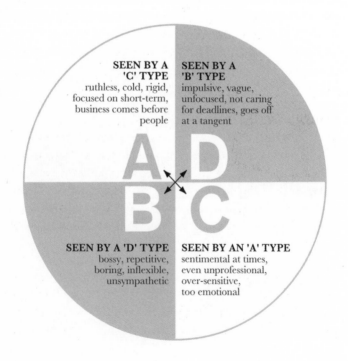

SEEN BY A 'C' TYPE
ruthless, cold, rigid, focused on short-term, business comes before people

SEEN BY A 'B' TYPE
impulsive, vague, unfocused, not caring for deadlines, goes off at a tangent

SEEN BY A 'D' TYPE
bossy, repetitive, boring, inflexible, unsympathetic

SEEN BY AN 'A' TYPE
sentimental at times, even unprofessional, over-sensitive, too emotional

Talent Pool

To innovate successfully we often need to employ and promote people who have different views and ideologies to ourself. Some respond well to anecdotes, stories, graphic representations and bite-sized bits of information. Others prefer hard analysis, bare facts and lots of statistical back-up. Being successful in business is usually about working with all types and often having the ability to tailor a pitch or message to the audience. This is a bit like being a work chameleon, someone who is able to discuss timetables with a delivery driver then go into the office to chat through marketing plans with a major client. Being able to do a great sales presentation one minute and also discuss performance issues with staff the next.

How well we succeed over a period of time might well revolve around the difference between how good our best skills are compared to how poor our worst area of expertise may be. If we were to list our three least effective work capabilities and look at how often we have to use them, it might frighten many. I have a friend who is a professional golfer, is highly talented and has had some real success on the European PGA tour. The extent of his achievements is more likely to revolve around how good the worst parts of his game are, compared with how good his preferred skills may be. Our strengths often take us into a strong position in the first place but after that it's about how we are able to handle our weaknesses under pressure or at really busy times.

Reactions

How we each react to different business situations and life experiences will also vary. Changing established views and procedures will cause conflict and often the management of this confrontation is the key to success during particular phases of our career. I certainly believe that an amount of tension is often a necessary requirement for change, innovation and creativity for most of us. Removing the comfort blanket is when we are most likely to develop new concepts, ideas and plans, inspired by the need for change. Many people take the process of adopting change too personally, feeling others are trying to undermine their authority or way of working and may effectively retreat to safe ground. This needs careful explanation so that alternative points of view are not putting others down, just looking for a way that everyone can improve.

A dimension that adds some complexity to this analysis is ability. Those with a greater weight of understanding, for whatever reason, usually have a deeper ability to influence others and drive a result along the path they wish. Differing abilities should not, however, reduce the need to understand our own brain balance and thought process. It should just add another tier to our thinking. The next time you are in an important meeting, try to judge who are right and who are left-brain thinkers. Establish which people are likely to agree or empathise with others, and therefore who will be more likely to form a consensus. This behaviour is rarely random at all but due to each individual's personality framework. Getting people on your side is about positioning your argument so that the message appeals to differing types. The people who go in strongly and firmly could easily lose support from more reserved or analytical people. Read the way conversation and exchanges of information go, as you may need to modify your usual and pre-ferred tactics in order to move things in the direction required. It's not always possible to achieve everything you desire in a short space of time but you can change people's attitudes to you and various arguments by positioning yourself differently. It's possible to make allies from enemies and effect change by simply bringing others round to your point of view.

Personal Profile – Harry

Background – having moved quickly through management ranks within the training and education sector, Harry became Managing Director of a successful company owned by one of the largest media conglomerates in the UK. He felt that working for big business took a lot of his natural energy, however, and increasingly it seemed the rewards did not outweigh the stress, pressure and impact on other parts of life.

Success – Harry was in his early forties when he went to his boss with the plan of taking a six-month sabbatical, giv-ing him the time to think about what the future might hold. He came to the conclusion on this journey that the reality of a lifestyle change was far less traumatic than the natural apprehensions of that course of action. Harry found the confidence in himself and the self-belief that he could cope with whatever was thrown at him. He sees that many of us put work and job-related relationships on some kind of pedestal, feeling that we cannot exist without those workplace colleagues. In reality, we rarely choose workmates, in the same way as we choose friends and much of the interaction is down to the fact that we are forced to spend a lot of time together and share a lot of day-to-day problems, rather than because we enjoy each other's company. As soon as we take everything related to our job off this elevated status, other decisions about our lives become so much easier.

Work Balance – our view of life is often biased as a result of placing too much importance on material goods rather than the quality of our lifestyle. Harry is clear in his own mind he would be happy to swap material things in return for being in greater control of his own life and making his own choices.

Retirement – he has started his own education company with several other work colleagues and also investing in an international property venture in the Far East. Retiring, in a traditional sense, seems no closer nor particularly desirable and he feels it is a phase where we should aspire to have more control over what we do, rather than actually doing less.

Advice – he encourages us all not to wait for that life-changing experience, which can often be a really bad life event and instead, take action when the time is right. Many of us put off making the tough decisions about changing occupations or dropping tasks that don't make us happy; these things rarely get easier as time goes on. One key route to greater happiness and balance is tackling the difficult decisions as quickly as possible. Sometimes this involves short-term pain but that is always positive, as we are at least moving in the right direction. If any of us can't see the wood from the trees, Harry believes a sabbatical from your job can be tremendously rewarding. This period can be more productive if we have managed to identify some key issues beforehand. Trusting others is important, as close friends and colleagues can offer good advice.

High-Touch

Daniel H. Pink, in his book, *A Whole New Mind – Why Right Brainers Will Rule the Future*, introduces the idea that we need to develop a new mindset based around high-concept and high-touch senses rather than traditional talents. He identifies the six senses as follows:

'1. Not just function but also DESIGN. It's no longer sufficient to create a product, a service, an experience, or a lifestyle that's merely functional.

2. Not just argument but also STORY. When our lives are brimming with information and data, it's not enough to marshal an effective argument. Someone somewhere will inevitably track down a counter-point to rebut your point.

3. Not just focus but also SYMPHONY. What's in greatest demand today isn't analysis but synthesis – seeing the big picture and, crossing boundaries; being able to combine disparate pieces into an arresting whole.

4. Not just logic but also EMPATHY. What will distinguish those who thrive will be their ability to understand what makes their fellow woman or man tick, to forge relationships, and to care for others.

5. Not just seriousness but also PLAY. There is a time to be serious, of course. But too much sobriety can be bad for your career and worse for your general well-being.

6. Not just accumulation but also MEANING. We live in a world of breathtaking material plenty. That has freed hundreds if not millions of people from day-to-day struggles and liberated us to pursue more significant desires.'

Application of Senses

Here are a few thoughts and notions about the application of these underlying propositions and the factors affecting the new mindset:

Design

Can you imagine a traditional business changing the colour and layout of its logo regularly like Google? Many undervalue the influence that design has on consumer reaction and spending, client behaviour and suppliers. Getting across a key message isn't just about putting it in front of people. I have seen many businesses become remarkably nervous of making changes to their logo, identity or marketing visualisation, seemingly concerned they will alienate existing clients or even make a communications mistake which will lead to costly retracing. For me, changing colour, textures, fonts, relative sizes and positioning, can be highly effective at getting across the change culture. It's also a statement of how confident we are. If someone hasn't changed their corporate look and feel in any substantial way for five years, does that mean that they also haven't changed their product or service levels or attitude? Not everyone can take the time required to go to design school, but we *can* keep a blank booklet in your pocket and sketch ideas whenever you have a spare moment. It just might be more productive than checking in with the office. Trying a variation on an existing identity doesn't have to lose customers and can attract new ones.

'Paul Smith's introduction into fashion was completely accidental. At the age of 16, with no career plans or qualifications, Paul Smith was propelled by his father into a menial job at the local clothing warehouse in his native Nottingham. Within two years, he was managing his first boutique and with the encouragement of his girlfriend Pauline Denyer (now wife) and a small amount of savings, opened a tiny shop in 1970. Paul started to take evening classes for tailoring and with the help of Pauline (an RCA fashion graduate), Paul was able to create what he wanted. By 1976 Paul showed his first menswear collection in Paris under the Paul Smith label. Within 20 years of his introduction to fashion Paul Smith had established himself as the pre-eminent British designer.' (Extract from fashion designer Paul Smith's website, paulsmith.co.uk.)

Story

Nike has taken a niche sports brand and told a story through its advertising campaigns that show how cool it can be to wear certain styles of clothing. It didn't just say it (which isn't cool in the first place), it let the classic art of storytelling do its job and in this case in a stylish and irreverent manner. There has been a growing trend away from emotional engagement to bland and often meaningless communications, which don't say very much at all. At the same time as Nike were putting together images, music and text in a compelling way online and offline, Disney was somehow moving away from its roots of wonderful story-telling towards an emphasis on action, special effects and one-dimensional impact. The recent fortunes of these companies could not be more different.

One of the businesses I started some years ago is heavily involved in graphic design, mostly operating in the media and entertainment worlds. We have retained many clients from its beginnings in 1998, because it tries to take people on a journey, showing how products and services, brands and websites evolve on a voyage of discovery. It is often fairly easy to come up with a number of different design concepts and hope that clients like them, but this can be a very hit-and-miss approach. It doesn't appreciate the fundamental experience of taking someone from where they are right now, to a different place. As an example, we were redesigning a series of journals for a medical publishing company and I was struck by how little the look had changed for some time. The client was very conservative and traditional but I remained convinced they would appreciate something more con-temporary, clean, confident and striking. I didn't expect them to take a leap from their current position straight away, however. The task would be to present a series of concepts starting close to the *status quo* and leading into the unknown. The only way to get my message across was for the client to fully understand and empathise with the process I was taking them through. As I presented each idea, getting further away from the comfort of home-base, they got more enthusiastic because they understood the road we were going down. They moved a long way (four steps out of five to be exact), which was due as much to the story as it was to the design.

Symphony

What Steve Jobs has done with Apple in his second stint, is nothing short of genius. Developing and releasing new products and services seamlessly into a competitive space, building the target audience each time, in an innovative and exciting way continues to captivate many people all over the world. He has managed to pull his disparate teams, from product design to engineering and marketing to technical services, into a single shared vision. Somehow they all were able to connect and see what could be possible.

I have always enjoyed playing and watching sport and it never ceases to amaze me how we all see things differently. Whether it's a golf shot from 100 yards over a bunker, a reaction volley close to the net or preparing to start a race, we are all going through the same process but in different ways. Some can see the bigger picture and focus on the things that matter, while others are always a step behind. That ability to keep the head up marks the difference between those who have time and others who are rushing to catch up. Business is very much the same; there are those who not only do their job but are able to see outside their immediate area and comfort zone. They can make connections, see how fusing disparate events or elements can be beneficial and combine things in a way that makes more sense. I am a great believer in the power of the arts. I realise that may sound a bit flowery but exploring creative and expressive disciplines has helped me keep my head up and look towards the horizon. I'm not sure whether sitting down and trying to paint would help everyone but having a place to store good ideas might just be useful.

Empathy

I called up Citibank to chat about opening a new account, having got really poor service from one high street bank. I was asked to call back by the first lady, was then told the person I needed to speak to was on holiday, and finally, politely informed someone would call me back. I'm still waiting! This is nearly as bad as waiting on the line for British Telecom (a telephone company after all) to answer their phones. This is another business with very little empathy for people when things go wrong. Let's face it, when something goes wrong and how that is dealt with is often the defining point in a business relationship.

I had someone who worked for me who was very good at their job but lacked empathy. Other people's shoes didn't seem to fit. It was as if a list of tasks was ticked off but insight and understanding of individuals weren't developing as they should. No real long-term relationship assets were being nurtured or built. Barack Obama, when referring to a Supreme Court appointment stated, 'We need somebody who's got the heart, the empathy, to recognise what it's like to be a young teenage mom, the empathy to understand what it's like to be poor or African-American or gay or disabled or old – and that's the criterion by which I'll be selecting my judges.'

Play

A recent Virgin Airlines ad campaign plays on the retro theme. It has lots of attractive smiley airhostesses in red uniforms walking side by side in slow motion while catchy music plays in the background. They sure looked like they were enjoying themselves. As I changed channels, a British Airways campaign was running. It showed a nice looking cabin, some clean looking seats and a plane taking off into the sunset. Pleasant, for sure but I wonder which one I would have more fun flying with?

There are many occasions in our working lives when we need to be serious, make tough decisions and really focus on some key aspects of our overall responsibility. Being like this the whole time, however, is neither nor ultimately good for us, the people around us, our work relationships (internal or external) the development of our career. It's easy to be upbeat and light-hearted when things are going well but it's when times are tough that we all need to be able to see the funny side, inject a sense of perspective or enable people to let off some steam.

I have been working with a large commercial glass company for several years and most of the meetings to discuss new ideas, marketing initiatives and creative things take place in a room with no windows and in an environment of dour efficiency. You wouldn't call it harsh or severe but certainly not very helpful for coming up with innovative solutions or trying to change existing ways of working. I decided to arrange a meeting at a completely different venue, a better rather than level playing field. I was trying to get people to think more expansively about their roles and markets by mixing work and a little play. We had a meeting in a bright, airy and interesting area, followed by lunch in a private room of a good restaurant and managed to get more creative input that day than in a dozen previous meetings. Most of the people still talk about the food, the service and what fun we had. It was as if we weren't actually working at all!

Meaning

Many of us have lost some of the meaning to our lives because much of our energy and natural mental activity has been galvanised by working routines. During my early twenties, I became quite obsessed with success and the pursuit of corporate goals over self-development and happiness. I struggled to enjoy the journey because I was pre-occupied having lost the reason for going to work in the first place. It took almost 15 years of working to see the light. I remain driven to achieve important things at work, but have been able to incorporate new experiences that keep me balanced and fulfilled. One of the problems for me (and a constant topic in my research for this book) has been the incessant pace of modern life. There are many possible ways to address this but any strategy needs to fit in with our life. One solution that works for me is a day of peace; no mobile phones, no emails, no television, no car. One day a quarter with time to reflect, read and write down some things that are important. If you can't make a whole day, start by setting aside a few hours as an aperitif.

The Dalai Lama has some words on happiness: 'I believe that the purpose of life is to be happy. From the moment of birth, every human being wants happiness and does not want suffering. Neither social conditioning nor education nor ideology affects this. From the very core of our being, we simply desire contentment. I don't know whether the universe, with its countless galaxies, stars and planets, has a deeper meaning or not, but at the very least, it is clear that we humans who live on this earth face the task of making a happy life for ourselves. Therefore, it is important to discover what will bring about the greatest degree of happiness'. If you can take ten minutes and visit dalailama.com, you will not be disappointed.

Lateral Thinking – No Such Thing!

Edward De Bono was primarily responsible for a veritable tsunami of new ideas and thinking starting several decades ago. Many people still use his approaches, exercises and theses to help foster a creative process. I have an issue with the whole concept of lateral thinking in today's workplace; anyone who isn't thinking outside the box or along new dimensions isn't, in my mind, thinking at all. Anyone who is plodding, one step after another, in broadly the same direction can hardly be considered to be going through much of a thought process. To think properly, we have to consider things outside the standard and into the realms of different, unusual and innovative. I remain, however, a big fan of De Bono.

In his book *The Happiness Purpose* he states, 'The proposed religion is based on the belief that the legitimate purpose of life is happiness and the best foundation for happiness is self-importance. The happiness purpose is to be achieved through the use of thinking and humour and dignity'. One area of his work that still has huge relevance today is recognising that happiness is a legitimate purpose of our existence. I left proper work (i.e. employed by a big business) wanting to see if there was a way of combining work with greater enjoyment of life and freedom of expression. I still needed to earn money and be part of a business or initiative that was rewarding but I also wanted to spend more time doing the things that were fun. It was about trying to have greater control over my life agenda. It took several years to completely remove some of the emotional chains of 'real' work and a good example is nipping off early in the afternoon. I spent many years thinking on sunny days how much fun it would be to get out of town and visit some friends and catch up on emails, etc. later in the day. Running my own show gave me that opportunity but I still felt like a sinner, like a naughty schoolboy playing truant. I didn't have any investors or shareholders to please, but there was still that guilty feeling that I was doing something very wrong by enjoying myself rather than toiling away in an office somewhere. It wasn't that I wanted to work for fewer hours, but just fit life and work together more harmoniously. The good news is that after years of practice, I may now be completely cured of that feeling of guilt!

De Bono believes that the pursuit of happiness is a question of balance. In our working lives we usually create parameters for this situation, usually called 'cut-offs' and 'trade-offs'. Both are absolutely vital to be able to steer ourselves through the minefield of emotional uncertainty and mental unknowns. We need to deal with these to challenge our own state of mind. Many situations provide constantly changing factors and information, ensuring that we also need to adjust our thinking on a regular basis. Getting it right once doesn't mean we'll be correct the next time. De Bono believes all this is predicated on action. Without that impetus we don't learn, experience or observe. Many of the most successful people I have known believe that making the wrong decision is often better than making no decision at all. We just hope that in the long-run, we make more good decisions than bad.

What Attributes Do We Have?

Understanding our own attributes is often more difficult than identifying the relevant skill sets of others. Being self-critical is easy and most of us go through times when we are heavily tempted to put ourselves down, which rarely helps. Looking at the attributes of successful people can, however, be enlightening when we try to apply them to our own talents. I have rarely seen successful operators who are very poor in certain areas; they can turn on the charm when it's required and equally analyse problems when such focus is needed. The following list comes from *The One Minute Entrepreneur* by Blanchard, Hutson and Willis and is the top 20 attributes of successful entrepreneurs:

1) Resourceful
2) Purposeful
3) Focused
4) Risk-taking
5) Problem-solving
6) Salesmanship-orientated
7) Visionary
8) Optimistic
9) Leadership-orientated
10) Ambitious
11) Innovative
12) Integrity-based
13) Adaptable
14) Communicative
15) Self-motivated
16) Strategic
17) Team-orientated
18) Determined
19) Curious
20) Balanced

Best and Worst

It might be a useful exercise to list your top five and perhaps the ones from this list you consider to be your weakest. On a separate piece of paper, try to list the top and bottom five for the company, division or department where you work. See if there are any glaring differences. The third part of this exercise is about what skills and attributes are needed going forward. If you expect a move or shift in talent requirements over the next few years, then it's good to get ahead of that curve and start thinking about where you might want to focus some training or at least, positive action.

Looking Ahead

I met a lady who works in a marketing and communications capacity in the National Health Service in the UK. I took her through the personal attribute process and she placed a lot of emphasis on team-orientation, communication, problem-solving, determination and resourcefulness which also fitted well with the expectations for her area. When looking at her career over the next few years, however, a very different picture emerged as the impact of private services increased the need for more distinctive marketing. Suddenly strategic thinking and a creative approach entered the list of talents required and it became obvious that a refocus was required. Shifting external factors can, and often will, play a major part in what skills we require. One of the keys for this lady was to understand that a major shift was going to affect virtually everyone in her team. The change process and skill change was going to be mirrored by others, but to differing degrees. This would, in turn, alter her position relative to others in the organisation.

Personal Profile – Steven

Background – this guy had his own successful construction company, but due to a bad personal accident, he had to wind it down. He had to learn quickly there were other things that could provide fulfillment to his life. He believes that a walk along the seafront on a windy day cost nothing and every time, he sees others who are enjoying every minute. He has a very active mind and in his dealings on the stock market, manages to beat average yield percentages every year.

Success – he believes we are fooled by media, social pressure and often those around us into believing that happiness is having a big house, a nice car, multiple television sets, expensive holidays and everything that modern lifestyle is expected to provide. He asks who is happier: the guy who spends most of his life in the office and after bills gets little money to spend; or the man who works far less, has much more modest possessions around him but who has a similar amount to spend? Part of success for him is being able to choose the hours and place of his work, the real cost of spending too much time at the desk is what we are missing when we are there.

Work Balance – I asked him about balance and got this reply, 'My first memories of achieving a happy life-work balance came with my older brother, who started life as a mechanic. He became self-employed and advertised himself as a mobile mechanic, going out to people's houses to work on their vehicles. I remember he would work up to a Thursday lunchtime, by which time he had earned enough money for all his bills, food, beer and clothes and that was enough for him. Then on a Thursday afternoon and all day Friday, he would be preparing his fishing gear. I remember getting ready to go off to school and he was off fishing on a warm summer day. I was rather envious at the time and didn't even like fishing! All his life, he has lived like this, once the mortgage is paid, the bills sorted and a bit left, that's all he needs.' There is a great lesson here for all of us: a big part in finding happiness is knowing how much is enough. Another aspect is how caught up we can all get in the supposed safety blanket of putting money away for a rainy day, rather than getting on with living life as we face it.

Retirement – Steven believes if the idea of retiring makes you happy then you should go for it, set a goal and work towards it step by step. This will provide great comfort, especially if things get tough.

Advice – wealth is not about how much is in the bank, it is about the quality of our experiences. It is not as easy to quantify, however, which is why so many of us focus on money rather than fully appreciating the good things we have.

Find a Mentor or Two

Find a Mentor or Two
Eric Parsloe of The Oxford School of Coaching and Mentoring believes that 'mentoring is to support and encourage people to manage their learning in order that they may maximise their performance and become the person they want to be'. Mentoring is a much under-used personal development and empowerment tool. It can be a highly effective way of assisting us expand and broaden our careers and thinking. It is essentially the coming together of two people, the mentor and mentee, who share time, honesty and mutual respect. It is now an industry in itself and many mentors have professional qualifications, good commercial experience and a desire to help. These are important traits but if the match is to work, the person must empathise with the mentees position and personality. Like any other relationships, each person must be able to identify with the other and their commercial experience.

Many mentors try to build confidence, provide guidance and also encouragement, giving the other person the ability to discuss key issues in depth. At times, I'm sure we would all benefit from being able to discuss complicated business or personal issues, which need to be resolved. I was given some

'At the heart of mentoring is the ability to become more self-aware and take greater control of our lives through a deeper understanding of our actions and preferences.'

advice early on in my career from a senior European HR manager who said the higher up the corporate ladder we go, the more isolated we can become. He believed senior executives are not encouraged to make friends within the company or with suppliers in the same way and need to be seen to keep their distance from many people in the business. They can't be seen to be having friendships that might bias their judgment or make others in the business question their reasoning. I wasn't totally in agreement with this piece of advice but did try harder to treat people more evenly and take more time to explain why I did certain things with people who I naturally liked.

One work colleague of mine became a mentor for a younger

person who needed help and counsel. That person did not know that he needed such help at the time, but both received many rewards from the process. Spending time with younger business people can open our mind to new ideas and ways of working, but also help to look at some of our own concerns and problems. As teachers, we can learn from the process of providing information and knowledge. Mentoring doesn't have to be on a professional basis (i.e. when money changes hands) and I know a number of people who confide in others for the exchange of ideas and interaction. If you know someone who might be able to help you, ask about whether they would like to be your mentor. What's the worst that can happen?

Here are my steps to get the most out of a mentor process:
1) Identify what kind of person you are looking for – what attributes do they need?
2) Timing – how often and how long do you plan to meet and discuss? It's tempting to try to 'meet' via email, Skype or video-conference but I never feel it works as well as face-to-face.
3) Content – build a list of things to discuss and rank them in order of importance.
4) Relationship development – a rapport isn't going to happen overnight so give it time to work. It's easy to say the person can't help because he or she doesn't understand me or my business environment but it's whether they can connect with you that is the key.
5) Schedule – try to meet in different places and at different times of the day. It can help keep both sides thinking.
6) New ideas – try to make sure you and your mentor keep the flow of new concepts and things to think about rather than just looking at the initial list.
7) Networks – it's possible that you can both benefit from each other's network.

Personal Profile – Carl

Background – from an early age Carl's energies went into making things and understanding how objectives were put together rather than traditional academic pursuits. He still sees great merit in this approach, applying it consistently to his various business activities and now runs a major leisure business.

Success – a significant achievement in his early career was overcoming the fear of getting things wrong and finding enough freedom to complete tasks the way he wanted to. Carl feels strongly that success is often about having the confidence to do things whilst building a strong base of transferable skills. That way, whatever is thrown at us during work, we can find a path. He also thinks that to be successful we need to expand our mental view and sphere of understanding, developing our senses to be more aware of what is actually happening around us, not what we think is happening. If we only mix with one type of person most of the time, we risk losing out on other perspectives and valuable points of view. Carl feels most of us have lost touch with our natural rhythm and this is because of technology and the pace of our working lives. Technology has made him more self-sufficient in business, which should be a big advantage but it has reduced his ability to spot opportunities because interaction. Carl has seen a growing trend of people believing success is measured financially rather than by the acquisition of skills. If we are predominantly money-focused, we are more preoccupied with how much we have, rather than enjoying the journey of our career. Many people he sees have lots of cash in the bank or material assets but are still insecure as individuals because they have lost track of what is important to them.

Work Balance – business is boring when it is quiet or when we are jumping through the same hurdles day after day, as we are not learning anything. He finds great balance from the adrenalin of new opportunities and finding ways to make things work.

Retirement – much of Carl's work doesn't feel like work, so he doesn't necessarily see any form of retirement being without what others would consider working tasks. He believes retirement is about having the freedom to make the decisions we want to make and do what we want to do, when we want to do it.

Advice – he feels getting more creativity and innovation into the workplace is often about allowing an attitude of openness to prevail and recognising the quality of thought, rather than necessarily whether it is entirely accurate. We all need to have mad thoughts now and again to remove mental inhibitions and to remind ourselves that answers can come from many different directions. He also believes we can all learn something about ourselves by improving our practical skills, as this is a way to change our approach to problem-solving. It's often a way of deconstructing work problems we face and building up solutions, one step at a time. He also feels we need to put time aside to look for things that make steering our ship easier. A good example is when we are working with people to sort out any problems or issues that are really urgent. It is a sure-fire way of winning trust and respect.

Reinvention

Changing business and personal circumstances is a fact of life. We often can't influence them to a great extent or see when they are coming, but we can be more prepared by getting into a mindset that is more open to evolution. For example, I have always believed the best way out of a crisis is to experiment and adapt; experiment by bringing new concepts in from outside, looking to adapt as many internal processes, procedures and systems as soon as possible. Making changes and improvements must become a normal and even expected part of your area of influence. This process is as valid for a small department or sole trader as it is for a multi-national conglomerate. A management style that embraces creativity, flexibility and responsiveness, relegating the fear of failure to the back row, will be admired and will provide tremendous encouragement to all concerned. This isn't a chance to stop looking at the detail or doing the basics well; every business needs to do these things consistently well but having the process of reinvention within will put you ahead of the chasing pack.

I have never met Larry Page or Sergey Brin, the founders of Google, but have read much about their amazing rise to stardom. In spite of their very different personalities and ways of working, they always provide a consistent front to employees, clients and suppliers. This is an amazing gift: an ability to see the bigger picture the whole time and to be disciplined enough to hold all those natural surging emotions in check. I would like to have just half of that!

Becoming Removed

Another way of looking at our working place state of mind is to examine the extent to which our energies are caught up in our day-to-day routines. I can remember long periods of time working for the Hollywood film studio MGM, flying all over the place, meeting after meeting, report after report, feeling removed from the customer and often the products I was trying to develop. It was a classic trap. I was doing my job but not really adding value. I was getting further away from what was happening at the retail level and in the supply chain but knew the first name of the concierge at a number of excellent hotels. The alarm bells were beginning to ring! One of my areas of responsibility was developing films onto DVD, something at the time which was quite challenging, as the technology was far from stable. The early adopters wanted a product that was new and exciting, packed with extra features but the market was moving much faster than anyone had anticipated and soon these products would be appealing to the mass audience. This group was much more price-sensitive and less concerned about a director's commentary or deleted scenes. To the annoyance of some of my senior execs, I re-prioritised my schedule to get closer to what was happening in the marketplace. This provided time to reflect and I decided to push for releasing two separate products simultaneously, targeted at different audiences to ensure we satisfied as many customer groups as possible. I managed to get reluctant approval on this new approach and it proved popular with the customers.

Personality Change

One business friend asked me whether I thought we could actually change our personality or behaviour; whether with training, encouragement and/or new stimulus, we could actually behave differently? I offered him my advice in the shape of two ideas. Firstly, we can change the perception of our behaviour, which is often what people are looking for. To be more open; make a connection; positive gestures, etc. Those things can be very conscious. I believe we can all evolve through reacting to the stimulus around us and as we get older we come into contact with very different people, places, music, films, etc. Our behaviour is underpinned by our thoughts and those certainly change as a result of these new situations. In fact, people who don't change and evolve must be ignoring the vast majority of things going on around them. The only issue is whether we actually recognise the personality changes that are happening in our sub-conscious or just put them down to getting older. Our behaviour is a key part of how we reference information to make decisions. It follows that as our instincts evolve, so do the paths we choose. We will therefore find ourselves over time in a different, much more fulfilled place.

Final Thoughts – Think Round Corners

Understanding how we think, how we are perceived by others and unlocking our store of creativity are major steps towards workplace success, happiness and fulfilment. We can be more fulfilled and accomplished not by working harder, but simply by thinking differently. Here are some of my favourite suggestions and topics from this chapter:

– Change will make some people apprehensive and nervous, so talking things through will save a lot of time in the long run.

– Identifying our own preferences, behavioural traits and judgments is key to making better decisions.

– Improving our communication skills is something that needs real focus. Understanding how different personality types interpret messages, could make a dramatic difference.

– We are naturally much better at certain elements of our job and improving on the weaker areas is a sure-fire way to add more value and be happier in the process.

– There is a need to be tremendously self-aware to understand how we instinctively react to change which will ultimately allow us to be more innovative.

– Finding a mentor and/or becoming a mentor can bring many benefits to our careers and workplace abilities.

– Establish the key elements of your work–life agenda, it will give you a career route map.

Random Mind Matter

* New ideas don't have to be life-saving or life-changing; even a small change in thinking can give us an edge or bring real benefit.

* Division of labour – one of the foundations of our industrial revolution was encouraging workers to specialise and break down work into discrete parts in order to do it more efficiently. Many companies today still operate this approach, some more consciously than others, so try to resist any move to pigeon-hole your role, especially if it means removing some of the fun stuff.

* Managing the Career - 'The effective careerist must get to know those inner forces which shape his or her needs and wants. These define personal identity, give direction, and add momentum.' Dave Francis, *Managing Your Own Career*. In the same book, the author lists nine career drivers:

'1) Material Rewards: seeking possessions, wealth and a high standard of living.

2) Power/Influence: seeking to be in control of people and resources.

3) Search for Meaning: seeking to do things which are believed valuable for their own sake.

4) Expertise: seeking a high level of accomplishment in a specialised field.

5) Creativity: seeking to innovate and be identified with original output.

6) Affiliation: seeking to nourish relationships with others.

7) Autonomy: seeking to be independent and able to make decisions for oneself.

8) Security: seeking a solid and predictable future.

9) Status: seeking to be recognised, admired and respected by the community at large.'

It is an interesting exercise to rank these in relation to your current working life. The other way is to look at how you might like to change the ranking ten years down the line in a perfect world to fit in more closely with your own personal characteristics.

* Car Parts – I was reading an article about the future of the automotive industry that smacked of out-dated thinking and practices. The global recession that mushroomed in 2008 and 2009, like all those before it, produced winners and losers. New car sales hit record lows, companies went to the wall and many jobs were lost.

There have been fears that many developed countries will lose huge employers unless they are bailed out by their respective governments. We have all seen pictures of endless lines of new cars with nowhere to go, sat in holding bays round the world and it seems to me many of the main protagonists have been stuck in the past, producing vehicles that are no longer wanted. The most recent recession certainly reduced demand for new vehicles but a tiny proportion of the car-mountain is made up of zero-emission, carbon neutral, electric or bio-fuel machines. The car industry has buried its head in the sand because developing these new products requires new talents. If they were really trying to embrace change and think differently, they would have spotted demand might go down as well as up and married that with a profound shift in consumer behaviour. Fewer people want, can pay for or justify large, expensive, petrol-guzzling vehicles, especially the younger people who have been schooled on environmental isues. This would have also saved the poor tax-payer as well, who has to foot the bill, one way or another, for the industry's inability to evolve.

'The fault, dear Brutus, is not in our stars, but in ourselves, that we are underlings.' William Shakespeare

4 Friends, Romans, Countrymen...

Aim

Very few people in business are able to achieve what they want without the aid of others, therefore building relationships, motivating, getting colleagues 'on side' and maintaining trust are all key elements for success. These skills are now even more necessary as our workplace fragments and careers evolve as a result. In this chapter we aim to look at and improve our people management skills.

'In writing this book I have discovered how many times in my life I have sought mentors: older people, to give me the benefit of their experience.'
Michael Parkinson, *Parky - My Autobiography*

Entrepreneurs

The vast majority of entrepreneurs I have met believe we have a better chance of success and happiness when working in partnership with other like-minded or complementary individuals. Rarely will we be able to maximise something new on our own and getting others on-board early is usually absolutely vital. Many of us have natural reservations about getting into business with friends, family or other people we know. I guess the issue is always if things go wrong the repercussions can be significant and affect a whole bunch of people. Looking at the downside is always a useful tool in business but shouldn't be the sole reason to dismiss potential useful relationships.

My experience has been different to many others. I have got into bed (in a business sense!) with many friends, colleagues, family members and acquaintances in areas as diverse as website design, property development, bars, television production and Internet start-ups. I have chatted long and hard with close friends about my key commerial decisions and asked them to provide valuable feedback. I have hopefully provided some help to them as well. My overriding consideration is a simple one: friends are people I like spending time with and work takes up a lot of time. When working with friends, I am going to spend more time with them. A win-win situation!

Golden Rules

There are, however, some golden rules of work/friend arrangements, the majority of which actually apply to any partnership you wish to establish:
* Demarcation – create clear lines of responsibility so everyone knows who is doing what.
* Contract – commit to paper the exact nature of the relationship and how income, costs, shareholding, assets, etc. are to be split.

The agreement may need to be altered or adapted after a period so try to leave room for flexibility. Rarely do new ventures pan out just the way we envisage so it might be worth putting a date in the diary for a regular review.

* Downside – make sure you have agreed what happens if things go wrong.

* Timeframe – identify the period for each activity and area of responsibility. Keep things in small parts, where possible.

* Money – most start-ups or ventures require some funding and cash means different things to different people. Over time the importance of money can change dramatically, especially if things get tough, so clear financial guidelines must be drawn up.

I'm sure this sounds like being too formal or over-doing what could be a simple venture or partnership, but if everything is nailed down in black and white, people know exactly where they stand.

The Bar Necessities

Some years ago I became involved in the bar business with a group of friends. The project was driven forward by one chap who was fed up with his career in the legal profession. Even though he was a partner in a reasonably-sized firm and was earning a good salary, he wasn't getting the kind of stimulation or fulfillment required from his existence. He longed to find something more enjoyable and creative giving him more flexibility in his life. Does this sound familiar? He identified an area of the pub/bar business industry that he felt was weak: few bars at the time provided the level of service that would create high customer loyalty. So, I and a group of close friends got together, put up some money and bought our first bar. The aim was to increase turnover substantially and then use the positive cashflow to acquire a second establishment. The business should ideally keep growing so it would have some leverage over the large suppliers and thereby improve margins. Many have tried, and failed, to make money from pubs, private bars, restaurants and the like, often because they think, as they spend time in these places, they know how to make them successful. The truth is that this business is tough, uncompromising and, at times, brutally hard work with long hours. It needs a special type of person who can work with a whole array of diverse personalities in order to be successful. And then there's the customer.

On the plus side, this kind of business does provide real autonomy and it isn't rocket science! We put outgoing, good-looking and cheery souls behind the bar and told them, this was their stage, not a cage. We spent time training staff and gave each of them a commission incentive. We wanted everyone to be rewarded if we were successful, after all the people serving drinks were the front-line sales force. I am still amazed at how many similar establishments I go into and, after what seems like an eternity, I am finally asked in a monotone voice by an unhappy-looking person, what I would like to drink. As with most business dealings, first impressions are everything and a smiley face along with a little personal interaction can make all the difference.

The first and subsequent bars that we acquired were in the West End of London and, like most other places in this area, had a real variety of clientele, from businessmen having lunch, to students meeting in groups, and couples having a quiet glass of wine. We felt there were three important groups of customers and identified them as follows:

1) Regulars – who visited often and drank the same thing most of the time. The aim was for all staff to know their name and drink.

2) Passing trade – sometimes in ones and twos but often small groups. The aim was to convert them to regulars and make them feel welcome.

3) Corporates – often dressed in suits or smart clothes, could turn up at lunchtime or directly after work. This group might spend more and often meet with clients, friends or work colleagues so the aim was to provide them with a comfortable, welcoming environment that was suitable for informal business meetings.

We decided to dedicate a couple of rooms as party areas which can be great business as having 50 people in a space for a leaving drinks, birthday bashes, etc. can be very lucrative indeed. It was important that these people, especially if they were spending more money, received good service. It doesn't take much for a member of staff to say, 'I'll bring your drinks over, go and find a table'. The customer feels good and a better relationship is often struck with that member of staff. We were not trying to offer varying levels of service, but we wanted to tailor approach to each group's specific requirements. As a further example, if a 'regular' comes in with a friend, we should make sure he feels at home. Regular customers in any business are much needed and should be viewed as potential salesmen and saleswomen. Often they do this unconsciously.

After several very good years and two further acquisitions, the business reached a critical stage. It either needed to continue to expand, and with that growth have a different sort of management structure or it would stagnate. Some of the other investors were happy to sit and watch what might happen, but I felt the 'hold' strategy was just not the right one. True to my instincts, I offered my shares to the others and got out. This meant that relationships were maintained and everyone was happy. The original vision had stalled because it was tough to continue executing the principles that started the business in the first place. Competition was also improving its game. The business did struggle (I wish I had been proved wrong) and lost its momentum and eventually completely fragmented.

> **'To be successful, you have to be able to relate to people; they have to be satisfied with your personality to be able to do business with you and to build a relationship with mutual trust'**
>
> **George Ross, Corporate Tycoon**

Personal Information

I was a big sports fan growing up and the individual that reshaped many hobbies into industries was Mark McCormack. As an enterprising American lawyer in the 1960s, he took three golfers and turned them into money-making machines through his company, IMG. He had a bit of luck as the guys were Arnold Palmer, Jack Nicklaus and Gary Player, three of the most successful and charismatic individuals ever to swing a club. His book *What They Don't Teach You at The Harvard Business School* is full of great anecdotes from his efforts to rewrite the rule-book but my favourite piece was actually about Mark himself. He would create a card for each business partner, associate or client and gather as much personal information as he could. Before meeting that person, he would have a look at the card and ask about the guy's wife by name, their children or the place where they live. Such gems of highly personal data, would make that person feel as though Mark really took an interest in them.

Personal Profile – Oliver

Background – Oliver is half French and half English and has risen quickly through the ranks in the film and music industries to become a senior figure and innovator in Europe. One of the biggest changes in his recent life was taking an MBA which included a three-month module on creative and personal mastery (CPM). I have included some more information on one such course towards the end of this chapter. It managed to alter his priorities from being very work-focused to having a better balance of family, work, hobbies and other things.

Success – he was, and still is, highly ambitious, although realises he is not going to get right to the very top. Having come to terms with this, he accepted this does not make him a failure, it just means he wasn't cut out for that role. He also now has a greater understanding that we can be ambitious without having to want more all the time, and that having other priorities, as well as work, doesn't make us care less about our career.

Work Balance – he looks to find success everyday, even in small things. A drive home from work where all the traffic lights are in his favour is very positive. Making something grow in the garden is another natural form of success. Lots of small changes can have a significant impact on our levels of self-fulfillment and self-esteem.

Retirement – the traditional view of retirement is not for him. Oliver would like a house in France and London, plus be able to do charity work, renovate old cars, help younger people in their working lives and remain very active. He sees his working life as a series of steps, moving towards not having to be dependent on the main salary. Each year he tries to get one step closer to those objectives.

Advice – Oliver states, 'ask yourself, if you get fired what's the worst that can happen? Life will not collapse'. He also believes we must all try to be one single person throughout

our work- and non-work life. As he has progressed up the
corporate ladder, he has talked less and listened more.
Suggests we should read, *The Art of Possibility* Zander and Zander.

Quality Service

During the 1970s, my father worked for the Trafalgar
House Group, which had at that time a remarkably
diverse asset base including Cunard (owners of the
famous QEII cruise-liner among others), construction companies and
The Ritz Hotel on London's Piccadilly. He managed to arrange
for an American business colleague to stay a few nights at The
Ritz and when I spoke to this New Yorker, he was very impressed
with the place. Several months later, the same man was coming
over to London and booked to stay at The Ritz again. He arrived
at the hotel with a client and walked into the reception. The
concierge warmly welcomed him using his name and said it was
nice to see him again. He was incredibly impressed (as was his
client). Now that's what I call service! In a few moments, a level of
service and a personal relationship was formed that went beyond
money or simply doing things well. That New Yorker never stayed
anywhere else.

Hidden Potential

Professor William James of Harvard famously stated,
'Compared to what we ought to be, we are only half
awake. We are making use of only a small part of our
physical and mental resources. Stating the thing broadly, the
human individual thus lives far within its limits. He possesses powers
of various sorts which he habitually fails to use'. I read this section
in Dale Carnegie's *How To Win Friends and Influence People* and it
still inspires me to think that we all can do so much more, if we
could only unlock some of the doors between our ears.

Confucious says, 'don't complain about the snow on your
neighbour's roof, when your own doorstep is unclean'. There is a
lot in this for surely all of our business doorsteps have some mess,
for none of us are a perfect commercial specimen. The urge to
change, regulate or improve others is very strong in us. I was very
quick to criticise in my early years at work and I must have been a
nightmare to work with. Looking back, I was trying to impress and

get along with all speed. It took many hard lessons to understand that it was more profitable to improve myself, than try to change others. I eventually understood that it didn't matter if I was right, that wasn't the point. Being right had nothing to do with it. Dealing with people is not about logic. It is more about emotion. We are all creatures that carry around with us briefcases full of pride and vanity, prejudices and sentiment. I had more than most. Dr Johnson said, 'God himself, sir, does not propose to judge man until the end of his days'.

Getting Things Done!

There are many ways of persuading people to do something but only one sure way: make the other person *want* to do it. We can promise much gold, threaten bodily harm or expulsion but actually motivating someone to feel they are doing things for themselves is an art form all unto itself. Getting people 'on side' is about giving them what they want. Some require money (which is often the easiest route) but most of us are motivated by many other

'In real life, friendship involves risk. The reward is great: help in times of need, joy in times of celebration. But the cost is also great: self-sacrifice, accountability, the risk of embarrassment and anger, and the effort of winning another's trust.' Roger Scruton, *Sunday Times* columnist

things, such as our name in lights, some recognition or simply the desire to be noticed. Others just want to feel part of a team, appreciated as individuals or important in certain circumstances. The fact that all of us are different makes motivating an art form, not a science.

Understanding the signals and people's different states, when it comes to feeling important requires endeavour and close study. We need to collect and interpret the signs we all emit in a normal day. 'I consider my ability to arouse enthusiasm among my people the greatest asset I possess, and the way to develop the best that is in a person is by appreciation and encouragement.' This is a quote from the hugely successful American businessman, Charles Schwab.

Flatter to Deceive

Flattery is often used instead of appreciation. I'm sure very few of the girls I've dated have been that impressed with a 'nice shoes' comment and made on its own, it would be sure to fail. The difference between flattery and appreciation is sincerity. One comes with much application of feelings and emotions while the other can slip out without either. If someone performs a task or project in an average way, how should we react? We could say well done in the hope that it might be better the next time or perhaps point out all the things that were wrong or missed. It's a fine line and the answer revolves not around our own feelings, but those of the other person. Appreciating the effort is a given and should always be the starting point, even though that person has been paid to put that effort in. We can't change the work that has been done, but we can influence the efforts of tomorrow, so appreciating what will make that person respond positively is the key.

I had a young chap working for me for a number of years who lacked self-esteem and confidence, especially when meeting up with clients. Any criticism from anyone was really taken to heart and would affect his work for days or weeks. His self-belief was quite brittle and I wasn't sure when we started to work together that it would last. The relationship turned one evening when we were at a party given by one of our major clients. The week had been a bit of a nightmare, goalposts moved and mistakes followed on several projects that this guy was managing. The client was very aware of the situation and my employee didn't want to go to this event at all. I decided there was only one way to go; having managed to drag him to the party, I got us some drinks and headed straight for our client. After minor pleasantries I said the problems were my fault but that we were working together to fix them and we would do so quickly. I said my eye had been taken off the ball and we would get it right going forward. My employee from that day felt that whatever problems were thrown at him, we would stand shoulder-to-shoulder when the dirt was being thrown. I think he needed to feel we were a team and his self-assurance improved along with his performance from that day. His confidence grew so much that he decided to retrain as a teacher, something he had always wanted to try. I lost a good worker – a small price to pay!

'It is the individual who is not interested in his fellow men who has the greatest difficulties in life and provides the greatest injury to others. It is from among such individuals that all human failures spring.' Alfred Adler, *What Life Should Mean to You*

Do People Really Like You?

Many people have confessed to me that they get nervous around certain types of person (the boss is a common example), which can lead to issues. When I was 30 I was made Managing Director of a media subsidiary of the Phillips electronics empire, which had around 35 staff. Most of the employees were older than me and it was the culture within the company to put their senior managers on some kind of pedestal. One of my main remits was to try to change the direction of the company and getting to grips with everyone's actual role and contribution was far from straight forward. The company liked to have complicated lines of responsibility with many people reporting to two individuals. I chatted to all the staff and most were not that comfortable with having detailed conversations about changing their responsibility and remit with one of the bosses. Some were nervous of this rather brash young upstart but slowly managed to come round. My aim was to wear down the preconceptions over a series of face-to-face discussions, many of which had to be progressed in very small steps. I had to adapt my natural style, which is probably much more direct, to help build trust and then be open to people's issues. I needed to become more aware and responsive and a close friend gave me some good advice; you can't listen and speak at the same time. The process took many months but by the end everyone felt happier about where they stood in the new structure and what was expected of them.

One facet of building and developing human relationships, particularly in commercial dealings, is that we really can't afford a day off. We have to learn how to be as consistent with others as we want them to be with us. I worked for a guy at a large film company, who was a real inspiration most of the time. He often challenged people's thinking in a good way, got into their heads and provided room for them to express themselves. When things got really busy, however, he struggled to do this in the same way. His moods would change and by the look on his face, some days you knew it was time to put any questions into the filing cabinet. Overall though, I thoroughly enjoyed working for this chap and respected him but learnt to pick my times and not always push ideas or proposals forward, even if the business really needed them to be moved on.

Do You Like To Win Arguments?

Do you sometimes try to win arguments that don't need a winner? If you do, then you are an arguer. Much of our frame of reference for heated debate stems from our childhood and early life. Sibling rivalry, peer discussions and potential responses, all helped shape our desires or otherwise to tackle issues. Most confrontations of this sort end up with each party being more firmly entrenched in their respective positions than when they started. A flow of emotion doesn't usually help us understand the other's point of view but just makes us blind to the fact that our own perspective may not be 100% correct. We must also ask ourselves whether arguments actually do any good in our workspace. There is no doubt that, at times, having the ability to let off steam can clear the air and get people talking but the line between a healthy and useful debate and an argument is a fine one. I like to classify this as a difference in listening: a good debate is when people obtain a better understanding of the other views while an argument tends to be more about just projecting an angle with some force.

Building Relationships

Many people have moved into property development as a business, which always seems like a strange one to me or at least an easy option for those who don't want to look very hard. Often with little or no experience of vital legislation, building regulations or with good trade contacts, many plough on regardless. It's a business with easy to understand fundamentals and there are virtually no barriers to entry. Banking institutions also actively encourage us to borrow vast sums, except in times when they are forced not too. I had an idea for purchasing houses or flats in very rentable locations, which for various reasons were not as expensive as others in the immediate vicinity. This might be because a property needed converting, redecorating, reconfiguring, restyling to modern tastes or was leasehold. What would underpin the value, however, was rentability and location is always key to this. If I could solve the problems, it seemed like a good venture.

Although I was able to find appropriate properties, I needed a partner who could handle other parts of the business. It would have been possible for me to buy them, get builders in and handle the whole thing but I didn't believe this was my strength. I was OK at managing the front-end stuff and some of the other issues such as the leasehold position but didn't want to spend vast swathes of time chasing tradesmen who had not finished on time or done what was requested. This required very different skills and an outlook that was probably a long way from my own. I found such a partner and a good business arrangement was created. Working with different types of people, however, can bring other issues, especially if your fundamental ways of working are different. The building works side of this business needed someone who had more experience in dealing with tradesmen and a better understanding of how the whole process would fit together. The approach I took in this venture was to establish very clear lines of responsibility and from the outset we worked well as a team. I avoided getting involved in his area and he didn't meddle in mine. Where we overlapped, I tried to set guidelines in black and white on both sides, so there was little

'There is great comfort and inspiration in the feeling of close human relationships and its bearing on our mutual fortune.' Walt Disney

room for misinterpretation. When things went wrong, and very few business dealings go completely smoothly all the time, I attacked issues one at a time and tried to put distance between discussions. One valuable lesson I learnt was to never say the other party is wrong, as it achieves nothing other than turning a debate into a less-than-productive heated discussion.

Personal Profile – Mary

Background – a German academic who moved successfully into recruitment (becoming partner) and heavily involved in individual personal development with senior corporate executives. She currently works for a large New York listed company with a pan-European remit.

Success – the feeling of having greater freedom and control over her schedule and routine is a big part of what success means to Mary on a day-to-day basis. Her academic background has helped her review her life and spend time thinking about what activities, both mental and physical, make her happy and fulfilled. Many senior managers she sees get drawn into the fast, very reactive world of commerce and subsequently don't find the time to mentally run through all the relevant personal alternatives and issues. A lot of what she works on with clients is attempting to put their business goals and personal requirements on the same page.

Work Balance – she made a big decision several years ago to address her work-life balance, whilst being courted by a major recruitment firm. After careful consideration she eventually agreed to join them but on her terms, wanting to work a 4-day week. She enjoyed recruitment but didn't want to spend all day, every day performing similar tasks. She felt lecturing and developing other academic studies was more important to her than having a larger salary each month. This was probably easier for her to do starting with a new company, than if she had been in the same firm for some time. She was surprised by some of her friends' reaction to this down-shift; many assumed she had become less serious about her job, which was indicative of how many view this kind of transition. She has seen a big shift towards longer working hours and is concerned for people who leave their mobiles or Blackberry[c] on all the time. She feels that many people haven't established a clear boundary for where work stops and starts, which is in sharp contrast to her German roots where many firms consider people are working too slowly if they have to be at their desk too long! Technology has made most parts of her job easier, especially doing business in multiple time-zones but this is only because she has set rules on usage.

Retirement – likes the activity of work along with the purpose it gives and would ideally continue to do some commercial things as long as she is able. For her, there are significant physiological merits in staying mentally active, doing tasks well and keeping interested in new things. Work often provides much more than we think!

Advice – being involved in a variety of workplace and social things can be rejuvenating to the body and mind. This might mean participating in new sports or activities, socialising with a mix of different cultures or getting out regularly into the country if you live in an urban area. It's making sure there is a counter-balance to how we spend the majority of our time both in and out of work.

Full Responsibility

There can be a great deal of satisfaction derived from admitting one's mistakes. It is a courageous and often disarming quality. I remember a big meeting with a DVD replicator who had been responsible for a series of errors, leading to a significant delay in getting products to retail shelves right across Europe. It was a mess and I was getting a lot of flack from my bosses. I met the guy in charge over lunch and he started by apologising, saying he would take full responsibility for the problems, and couldn't blame anyone in his organisation or beyond. His honesty was very refreshing and the entire discussion revolved around how we could improve the process and rebuild the relationship that had been fractured. It was actually a turning point, as we didn't fight about why such mistakes could have been made in the first place but just looked at how to move on. The performance did improve and a better level of trust was the result.

Companies Don't Have Ideas, People Do!

Many firms I have worked with have tried to inject more drive into their operations by hiring bright individuals. The problem is that very bright people can also bring a whole raft of new issues and often lack the practical experience of how to get jobs done in the best way. If you are thinking of starting something new or bringing in some outside talent to add a dimension, it's often worth pausing to look at the impact this might have on the whole business. The right person for the job may not be the best or smartest candidate!

Warrior Spirit

Some years ago I worked with a media company who always tried to hire people with a real warrior spirit. The founder had this trait and saw great merit in trying to instill his ideals across the entire workforce. It was funny looking into the business from the outside as half the people were really not warriors at all. They might have tried to dress like it, but they certainly didn't think like it. The company was really like two beasts fighting against each other on a daily basis, trying to superimpose a culture on each other. My own approach to hiring people is that character should rank above credentials.

I was given a great bit of advice by a senior personnel lady about the art of recruitment. She said that when you're looking for someone to work with you shouldn't look for the right answers, but the right attitude. I was in my early thirties at the time and it took me about ten years to fully comprehend what she was talking about. I then started to look for openness, energy, curiosity and a willingness to learn rather than formal qualifications. Since then I have paid less attention to exam results or certain areas of experience and more about what's going on in that person's head and their heart.

'Hell is other people.'
John-Paul Sartre

Now Move the Goalposts!

Trying to get greater creativity in oneself, those we work with and others we deal with isn't always about having a well-oiled machine in place. This may sound paradoxical but more often than not, it is true If things are running smoothly all the time without a hiccup, we can become complacent. Sometimes changing things around or being a bit of a trouble-maker can bring new reactions, ideas and perspectives. Being innovative on any level often happens when our minds are made to act in uncomfortable or new surroundings. I'm not a big fan of outward bound, paint-balling or any of those team-building exercises, but shaking things up a little can have good effects. Trying to act in an unconventional matter won't happen on its own, having the right environment for people is the catalyst for change. If you believe that the way to do your job better in the long run is to come up with different approaches, then work out what structure is needed and then sell it to the boss. If you can't sell it to the boss, there's only one thing for it. *Become* the boss.

A Person's Reach Should Always Exceed his Grasp

Completing what needs to be done is usually dependent upon getting support and co-operation from others. Technology has replaced some of our face-to-face contact at work, making our ability to communicate effectively over time even more difficult. Many people spend a great deal of time with colleagues and yet know very little about each person's feelings, desires, motivations and even basic likes. It is as if those people enter their workplace and put on a blindfold. You might expect then that putting in place systems to address this would help, but in my experience, the companies that have regular appraisal systems to try to encourage this kind of insight, achieve very little. Often it can be worse than having nothing – it's very easy to hide behind an appraisal. Getting candid feedback and being able to look inside someone is about having the desire to do so, not just because we're told to by someone 'on-high'. The feedback process usually works well when it's a mix of formal and informal; a combination of having a drink after work, discussion within meetings, shared presentations and emails. If someone is struggling to provide feedback, then trying to get to the bottom of the cause can help on all fronts.

Professional Advisers

Professional advisers such as solicitors, accountants, management consultants, technical advisors, IT guys and the like tend to be viewed in one of two ways. The first is to think they are all out to earn as much as they can from you, for as little work as possible. The other is to accept they are a necessary part of life. If we take the position that we all need professional advisers at some point or other, then it's about finding how to get the best out of these relationships. Keeping costs down is a given but most professional people have good networks. Like any other business partnership, persuading them to feel more part of the business can only be beneficial in opening up new areas of commercial interest. You never know, at some point you might really need their help and that's when the value in the partnership will became clear.

Rubbing Shoulders

I have met a bunch of people in the media sector who seem to have the constant ability to know people, not just any old person but those who are highly sought after or very useful in many business areas. It's easy to say this is simply about charisma or being in the right place at the right time, but it is usually more about that person putting a greater value on these relationships than others. They work harder at the personal side of things and look out for other people's interests as well. There are certainly many ways of losing people's interest or turning them off. As an example, I am a lousy teller of jokes and consequently never tell them. I like people who are upbeat, optimistic and cheerful and often find this helps form a bond with just about any-one. I was at a book launch with a client and the famous British PR guru, Max Clifford, was there. People seemed a bit in awe of him but I went straight over with a smile on my face and said how much fun I was having. It turned out his company had organised the event and he gave me a personal tour. A connection was made that just might be of use some day.

Bad News

There are many ways of breaking bad news to staff, suppliers, business partners, etc. but far fewer if we want those people to remain on our side. This is rarely going to be an easy or straightforward thing to do: giving people information that they really don't want to hear or are not expecting can require very particular skills. I have seen people take the direct approach, with all-guns-blazing and others almost apologetically trying to outline something that really needed to get sorted. On one particular occasion, I had to make many people redundant from the same company. I wasn't looking forward to it but knew it had to be dealt with as the business was making big losses and haemorrhaging cash. I asked half a dozen friends who had quite varied commercial experience for their advice and got a full array of answers – everything from take your time to get it over with as quickly as possible. An HR guy said that once you have told someone they don't have a job anymore, they won't take in much else. This was true for most of the people. I was told to explain this was a company-wide situation and not down to any individual's personal performance and this certainly helped. In the end, I decided to deliver the news in the way that was true to me. I wasn't their friend before and wouldn't be their friend after. If there was a way to help, I would do so and wanted them to know I was truly sorry for the position they were in.

Personal Profile – Michael

Background – highly successful distribution and logistics expert mostly in the media sector, he has spent much of his life for large multi-nationals. He works closely with colleagues from America and mainland Europe, enjoying the challenge of aligning cultural norms and behavioural differences.

Success – Michael got to a point in his forties when things got more difficult. Success at work was driven by a strong bread-winner mentality but this was forged at the expense of time with his family and friends: he had little social life. The driving force behind the long working days to a large extent was to earn money to provide a better lifestyle for his family, but later realised that he hadn't stopped to ask his kids, wife, etc. whether they would have preferred him to be at the school sports day as opposed to perhaps having more nice holidays. The early part of Michael's life was very work-focused, providing a great source of self-fulfillment which came with promotions and more responsibility and he now firmly believes this is a self-perpetuating cycle. It's the idea that success at work brings more money, which provides a better lifestyle for himself and the family, so you need to become even more successful. As if success perpetuates success, rather than happiness. If he knew then what he knows now things would have been very different. More balance and less single-minded career time, would have, in all probability not affected his professional status but would have given back a lot of personal benefits.

Work Balance – like lots of other conscientious employees, he has developed a capacity to work for longer hours and under great intensively. This is a common pattern: as we work more, so our threshold rises. One of the biggest influences in his working life has been the attitude of others around him and for many years colleagues spent ten to twelve hours a day at their desks, setting a benchmark for others to follow.

Technology – Michael believes that his PDA is an essential part of his job and many modern communication devices can help a great deal. The issue for him is, 'who is in control?' If the technology is running our life, then it's like handing control to someone or something else. He has to fight the growing expectation for him to be available and responsive just about all the time. Although he can't run his operation without the new tools, there are clear rules about how they are used. He actively discourages calls after 6pm and asks clients and colleagues to text him, if something is urgent. He then responds to those messages when he wants. Michael feels that we need to apply the same level of discipline to technology as to other parts of our working life.

Retirement – Michael looks at this phase as two inter-related parts. There is financial retirement, and then there's the work side. Having enough money to exit from the main job is often about kids, lifestyle and expectations but retirement from a career is not about giving up working. For him, it is about having the choice to do what he wants to do. He would consider getting to a point of doing something else, even if it was a manual or relatively easy task, if it gave him more time to do the things he enjoys. He asks himself the question 'what he is retiring from?' He still wants lots of social interaction and it is always good to have some money coming in but having the ability to choose is what is key.

Advice – he likes one of the American ex-General Colin Powell's mantras, 'we mustn't confuse professional status with personal status'. Even though we may have a big title on our office door, we don't carry that status in our private life. When not working, we are just the same as other people. He also feels that big events, such as deaths, health issues, etc. are the time to break things up, bring in the new and look at what is really important. However, these events often happen when we get a bit older and making career-changing decisions are much easier when we are younger as this gives us the time and space to make a real difference.

Networking

I have put a section on networking into the people chapter for one reason: networking isn't about attending the odd trade show, online business forums or social events, it's about people. It's about understanding that individuals bring opportunities of all shapes and sizes as long as you are able to have the sort of relationship that brings those things into the open. A good example is in the job market, as many vacancies still don't get advertised, people ask for recommendations from trusted colleagues and a call goes out. Even if you are not actively looking for a new job, to have the sort of rapport that brings opportunities will put you ahead of the game. If you are not getting positive feedback or insight from those around you, then it's definitely time to reassess the state of your business network. You may not be as good as someone else but if you hear about things first, you will get ahead.

When I have moved jobs, it has often been because there has been a corporate reshuffle, a change in direction or some kind of structural adjustment. Usually this has led to many people either being let go or left with responsibilities they didn't necessarily want. I have always taken a very active stance in these times, both with trusted colleagues and those who work directly for me. Through my network of contacts, I have been able to help many individual's access third party organisations, get into new positions or in some cases, even set up their own business. I enjoy being able to give a little back but there is also a strong commercial logic that underpins these actions. A new level of trust and understanding is developed and results in the network becoming larger. This means the number of people with differing skills and talents that I can call upon, grows and with it, my ability to get a great many business tasks done. Still to this day, I get people call or email me saying they have a problem and can I help. In the vast majority of cases, I am able to put them in touch with someone else or give them some advice, which moves them forward. In return, when I have a problem, there are doors to knock at. That's the power of networking, when it works.

I once started chatting to a very attractive lady at a government-run function, and after five minutes was already looking for the escape hatch. I made my apologies and headed back to the colleague I had come with. The person asked the reason for my swift return and said that I'd just had my personality and behaviour interrogated. It felt like I was about to be arrested for crimes of personality! Any approach needs to be positive but also engaging, not scary or intrusive. Being memorable is great but being remembered for the right reasons is better.

Successful networking isn't about the number of business cards we have or the size of our contact list, it's about the quality of those relationships. That is a function of the connection that has built up and the personal link that has formed. I meet many people who are hell-bent on getting my business card before providing any tangible reason why I would want to have a commercial relationship with them. Invariably I find that I don't need a relationship like this, I can do most of the things just fine, so it's about whether I really want to strike up something new. I met a printer recently who seemed nice enough and we had a very affable meeting over a coffee. I left feeling that business came first and people trailed a long way behind his desire to meet targets. I haven't placed any business with that guy.

I have a friend who is a master at networking, really impressive to watch. His belief is that it's like matchmaking; like a game where two people are looking to connect but often don't quite know it yet. If this is the case, I have always felt relationships need something concrete to work on, if they are to prosper. Discussing things that might happen, hypothetical possibilities or some future event doesn't build bridges. We need to find a way to see how both parties can benefit and understand how the other works. Identifying something creative and taking it a stage further, even if it eventually doesn't make huge profit or benefit, does allow the people to be involved in something genuine and authentic.

Rob Yeung, the author of *The New Rules – Networking* **states, 'People who succeed not only produce results, but also ensure that others know about their good work, by creating a profile for themselves too. Having lots of people know you and like you will put you in good stead when it comes to handing out promotions, or thinking of people to put onto interesting new projects.' This is sad but true!**

Final Thoughts – Start the Journey

Many of us labour under the preconception that we need to do amazing or earth-shattering things to be happier and more successful. A simple, straightforward step, however, is to improve the quality of our workplace relationships. The impact of our business network will tell us a lot about whether we need to place more effort in this essential area of commerce. Here are a few summary thoughts from this chapter:

– Discuss your key workplace issues with trusted work colleagues and friends. Try a different approach and viewpoint as often as possible.

– Explore the possibility of starting a commercial venture of any kind of project with a friend or two.

– Look more closely at the sort of decision-maker you are, not just when things are going well but in all business states. See what impact your behaviour has on others around you.

– Build bridges whenever and wherever possible.

– Try to remove as many of the unnecessary processes or procedures that don't add real value to your business relationships. This will make room for new thinking to flourish.

– We can all improve and develop our network, and try to split it into sectors, following the key aspects of your business life.

– Get greater connection with people, engage don't interrogate, be positive but don't overwhelm.

Random Mind Matter

* Room to Think – many thrive in situations of flexibility and informality and I am certainly one. If this applies to you and your work colleagues, the issue then becomes how best to manage your goals and integrate them. There is little point in achieving great things, if others don't want to work with you or are continually resentful. Power is much more about influence than position: a fact that is truer now than ever before. More resources or a flashy company car are not the keys to innovation – freedom is. We need to find a way to somehow remove or decrease the restrictions imposed on us in our working life. Creativity is often a messy, unpredictable process and the sooner we try to make it neat and tidy, the more we may stifle its very essence. For the people I have met, the first step is about removing as much of the existing work clutter as possible, leaving room to create something new.

* Creative and Personal Mastery (CPM) – many educational establishments now offer courses on CPM and something like this could help you connect with new thoughts. Professor Srikumar S. Rao on the website areyoureadytosucceed.com outlines the aims of his course:

'Description: This is a course on 'creativity', about the human mind and its immense potential and how you can harness it to achieve your own ends and whether those ends are worth achieving. To reach any major goal you will probably need the help of others, so we will study leadership and the qualities of a leader. Most of all, this course is designed to help you discover your unique purpose for existence. At the very least it will get you started on this quest. The exercises prescribed are drawn from varied disciplines and many have their roots in different ancient traditions. These exercises produce results and have been used and refined by such eminently hard-nosed bodies as the United States Armed Forces and trainers of Olympic athletes. The course also deals explicitly with issues such as developing personal values, ethics, integrity and achieving mastery. A particular focus is the understanding and resolving of conflicts between personal values and workplace actions.

Objectives: The course has four principal objectives:

1) To expose you to a wide variety of techniques and exercises that have been found to be helpful in sparking the creative process; to help you select those that best fit your personality and apply them to many different business and personal situations.

2) To help you discover your 'purpose in life', the grand design that gives meaning to all of your activities; to help you find that to which you can enthusiastically devote the rest of your life. When you are moved by deep inner conviction is when you have the greatest opportunity to sway others, in short to become a 'leader'.

3) To show you how you can mobilise resources to reach your goals most efficiently. There is a non-linear relationship between 'work' and 'results'. Immense exertion can produce little outcome and, at other times, a little effort can yield a huge payoff. If you have an open mind you can learn to create serendipitous opportunities.

4) To enable you to find and achieve the balance in life that is right for you. Stress levels are rising in our society across all ages and occupations. It little profits you to achieve any goal if you are a nervous wreck during or after. There are always tradeoffs between accomplishments and price paid but they are not necessarily obvious. It is important to learn how to strive mightily while remaining serene.'

Even if this sort of course isn't for you or would take up too much time to be practical, I do believe that most of us need fresh stimulus in order to change our aims, goals and ways. To influence our work-life balance, we need to somehow cast off some of the old traits and leave room for new ones to take their place.

* Controlling Chaos – Romanus Wolter, on the website, entepreneur.com has some advice:

'1. Take time to re-energise your mind. When life seemed crazy during my childhood, my grandma would always say, 'You need a change of pace'. We would do something entirely different with no particular purpose, freeing our minds from constraints. Schedule 10 minutes a day as a 'mini-vacation' from tackling your action items to gain new perspectives. Listen to music, meditate, or take a walk. Your body often gives out when it is exhausted; your mind acts in much the same manner. Give it some downtime from the daily commotion you encounter.

2. Establish a pattern of game-changing behaviour. Letting go of

entrenched positions helps you gain perspective on possible new approaches. Schedule a specific time of day, maybe early morning or lunchtime, to think creatively. Begin the process by acknowledging how new developments may affect your business. Remove any doubtful thoughts from your mind, and pledge to figure out new ways to achieve your goals.

3. Remind yourself that you're a risk-taker. It took courage to start your own business. And as your business grows, you will become more and more secure in your decision-making. When new challenges occur, recapture your original entrepreneurial energy by allowing yourself to feel uncomfortable. Reinvigorate your risk-taking by investigating imaginative ways to move to your next level of success. Just acknowledging that there is a way out of any difficult situation increases your energy and lays the groundwork for new innovations.

4. Permit your experience, knowledge and intuition to provide your next step to success. Clarity and resolve are only thoughts until you act upon them. Your entrepreneurial spirit is your most valuable asset. Taking action rekindles your passion to conquer any new challenge. Begin by clearly defining the challenge in writing. This visual image makes the situation manageable and, therefore, resolvable. While you may not have all the information to solve each problem immediately, stay open to new ideas and methods, and your resolution will surface.'

5 Make a Giant Leap

Aim
In this chapter we explore how better work experiences can lead directly to a more fulfilled life. We will look at how others tackle new business opportunities and making that first vital step towards greater control. After all, being better in business and achieving more of the aims we set out to achieve in the workplace, can only make us more happy!

'Anything is possible.'
Barack Obama

Limited or Employed

If you are considering setting up your own business, there are a number of options to consider. The first alternative is whether to create a limited company or open the doors as a sole trader. Having a company certainly can add value from a number of perspectives, most importantly appearing credible and permanent to big companies. Opening bank accounts for any new venture is much easier when you show your memorandum and articles of association outlining you as a director and so on. Any good accountant can set up a limited company in a week or so without much expense.

The second alternative is to be self-employed and act as a sole trader which is the best option if the scale of the business is likely be limited to just you. A third option is to set up a limited liability partnership (LLP). This is favoured by many firms of solicitors as it limits personal liability to the share capital of the business (like a limited company) but allows for more flexibility to bring associates or outsiders into the fold. There is a fourth route that can also be useful which is to establish a new arm or division of an existing limited company. For a slice of the action or a deal which involves using someone else's infrastructure, you could formalise some kind of partnership and really hit the ground running.

Limited or Not

The factors that affect this decision are as follows:

* Credibility – when I left a 'proper' job to set up my own business, I immediately formed a limited company. I wanted to do business with some big, established corporations and to appear immediately credible. The corporations were reassured by my company number, registered address and VAT documents and it also made employing people easier.
* Upfront costs – setting up as a sole trader is usually the cheapest option and after a quick letter to the taxman, you are ready to roll. There is also nothing to stop you starting as a sole trader and then creating a company later, if business really begins to move.
* Scale of the business – if your venture is likely to operate on a small scale, then the benefits of having a company or LLP are unlikely to be that important.
* Expansion – growing a venture which is an LLP or limited company

is often easier as paperwork will already be in place. Adding extra partners, directors or issuing additional share capital can facilitate expansion plans easily. Raising investment for virtually every route is easier as a limited company.

* Ease of operation – when going out on our own, making things easy is one of the most important and underestimated factors. An LLP can be quite cumbersome to establish and usually limited companies can offer sufficient flexibility to cover what we want to do. It also forces the issue of getting an accountant on board which can help with the money side of things. If they are not friendly, helpful and value for money, fire them and get someone who is.

* Tax – the tax implications need consideration, as keeping tax costs as low as possible is vital. There may be some tax breaks at certain times for new businesses and generally some government help as well. Often a limited company can more easily claim back costs like VAT and other things.

* Liability – if your venture is risky and requires significant funding from others, it may be that being a limited company is more attractive as risk is (generally) limited to the assets of the business and not you personally. This is different where personal guarantees are concerned – these should be *avoided at all costs.*

* Partnership with others – whatever entity is most suitable, it is always beneficial to have enough flexibility to change direction, add partners, offer a share in the business or equity as guarantee, easily. Things rarely work out exactly as we all would like or had envisaged and new people or partners can keep a business growing.

Lots to Learn

Still wet behind the ears, I went to work for the media arm of The Virgin Group. My exposure to big business was a year placement with American Express and a similar time at the head office of the retail giant Marks & Spencer. I really wasn't sure wearing long trousers was for me, but, all this was about to change. I remember one of the first projects I became involved with was at Virgin's book publishing arm, which was then quite small and extremely unprofitable. I had to look at the business, the people and how some of their competitors were doing things to see what could be done. One day Richard Branson strolled into our office and asked about the subsidiary, I kept very quiet, being totally in awe of this god-like figure. Branson suddenly turned to me and asked my view. Everything went quiet and I wasn't sure I was going to be able to speak at all. Eventually I managed to blurt out that I didn't think the business would ever make money at its current operating level. It needed to grow to have any chance of thriving in a marketplace that was becoming more competitive and increasingly global.

The discussion went round a bit and covered some financials that didn't seem to make a lot of sense to me but he then asked me how I thought the business should grow. It felt as though this was a defining moment in my career to date. There was a burning temptation to utter the first thing that came into my head but the truth was I really didn't know how this could be achieved and said so. I was expecting Branson to walk off to find someone who did, but to my surprise he didn't know either and asked me to find out. I couldn't believe that anyone at this level would take any notice of someone so inexperienced. I dashed around for a couple of months and came back with a plan to try to buy some assets and small businesses to broaden the base, get some new

'Success is to be measured not so much by the position that one has reached in life as by the obstacles which he has overcome.'
Booker T. Washington

authors in keeping with the Virgin brand (music and entertainment rather than phones and broadband at the time) and bring in some new people. To my amazement, that's pretty much what happened.

Corporate Culture

Working for Virgin back in the colourful 90s, when it was a very different organisation from what it is today, was an unusual experience for me. There was an incredibly distinctive culture that ran right through the disparate and varied companies. It didn't seem to be written down or overtly expressed by anyone. I thought it was a secret that I needed somehow to find out but, in fact, it was all down to attitude. If my behaviour and approach to business and life mirrored that of the Virgin way, I would get on with people and share in the success. In Branson's book *Business Stripped Bare*, he talks at length about this phenomenon and I've pulled together 25 core values and ways of working that strike a note with me:

'1) At its heart, business is not about formality, or winning, or the bottom line, or profit, or trade, or commerce, or any of the things the business books tell you it's about. Business is about what concerns us. If you care about something enough to do something about it, you're in business.

2) Business is creative. It's like a painting. You start with a blank sheet of paper.

3) There are many ways to run a successful company. What works once may never work again.

4) Business has to give people enriching, rewarding lives, or it's simply not worth doing.

5) Avoid taking on someone else's legacy.

6) There's no rule-book. The past is the past.

7) Put people together in a way that will have them bouncing ideas off each other, befriending each other, and taking care of each other. Suddenly they will be coming to you not with gripes and problems, but with solutions and great ideas.

8) Listen more.

9) Allow yourself and those around you to feel good about what you and they do.

10) I find it extraordinary that so many managers pay no attention to the fabric of their workplaces. How are people supposed to believe in a company when all they see of it, day after day, is a couple of pot plants and a fire extinguisher?

11) Encourage people to take ownership of the issues that they confront in their working lives.

12) Remember who you are: it's the biggest challenge an expanding business ever has to face.

13) Circumstances and opportunities change. Come to terms with the fact that the world changes – the only constant is change itself.

14) The more you free your people to think for themselves, the more they can help you. You don't have to do this all on your own.

15) Befriending one's enemy is a good rule for business – and life.

16) Publicity is absolutely critical.

17) Don't promise what you can't deliver, and always deliver everything you promise.

18) It is attention to detail that really defines great business delivery.

19) Success one day doesn't give you a free lunch every day thereafter.

20) Keep a cool head.

21) Never do anything that means you can't sleep at night.

22) Don't try to deal with it all by yourself. Don't be afraid to seek help and advice. If someone else is better than you at dealing with it, then delegate it.

23) Don't be afraid to make mistakes.

24) Innovation is what you get when you capitalise on luck, when you get up from behind your desk and see where ideas and people lead you.

25) You only get one chance (at life).'

Personal Profile – Alex

Background – from a good public school upbringing Alex quickly progressed to being a city fund manager and seemed to have his career sorted by his late twenties. Even at this tender age, however, he realised the obligations of this kind of vocation were too great for him. He left the safe and well-paid corporate world and set up his own consultancy with the aim of achieving work and personal goals simultaneously.

Success – achievement for Alex is working in an environment that offers stimulation and challenge, whilst being able to do things that are of real interest. Having been exposed to the world of banking, he found the atmosphere very political and cut-throat, with few people having any time for others they worked with. It was as if the nature of their work put blinkers on many people in that environment. Success, in his own venture, is now focused on retaining a small number of good clients whilst trying to explore new areas of business in order to find out more about himself. On a broad scale, self-fulfillment is about finding a harmony between work and his social existence.

Work Balance – Alex is an early adopter in many areas of technology and always looks to see how he can improve the quality of his life, by not just being able to push a few buttons in order to get tasks completed a bit quicker. Improvement is about combining efficiency and adding lifestyle value. He would like to start one or two other ventures, far away from finance, ideally something that helped others or the environment. He is not a natural risk-taker or entrepreneur and would need to feel comfortable with business partners and how interaction with outside firms would be structured. His career needs to be built one brick at a time.

Retirement – after some thought, Alex felt that retirement should be defined as a period when we are able to get our work-life balance absolutely right. Traditional retirement as it was once known could well be impossible unless we have plenty of money set aside. He is therefore reserved about making many predictions about a phase of his life that he feels he can't really influence a great deal for some time.

Advice – if we are able to learn something new every day, we will not only feel as though we are moving forward in our business activities but also have more opportunities available to us. If we go through a period when we are just doing the same things, our mind-set can quickly become very conservative and lazy. He believes if we define what drives and motivates us, we are half way to achieving success and fulfillment.

Think Service

I have always enjoyed the British coastline and, in particular, Devon and Cornwall. It's so rugged, unspoilt and different to just about any area in the world that I have set eyes on. In August 2004, torrential rains caused major flooding in many parts of the UK but the pictures that came back from the small village of Boscastle were amongst the most spectacular. Cars being washed down the valley towards the sea, houses with fast flowing rivers running out of control on both sides of them and lovely old stone bridges being completely destroyed. One of the best hotels and bars in the town is called 'The Wellington' and soon after the floods they set about restoring the 400-year-old coaching inn back to some kind of normality. The TV presenter Laurence Llewelyn-Bowen lives in a nearby village and agreed to redesign the dining room, which now looks fantastic. The point to this rather long and rambling story is about service. The place has great views down the valley and even in winter offers a magical outlook over the stream, gorse, angled trees and small fishermen's cottages that line the village. For me, service has always been linked to expectation and value. This place has a fantastic-looking dining room and city prices, therefore you expect great service. Simply having a great view isn't going to bring punters back.

My own dining experience in these lovely surroundings didn't start well as the receptionist had lost the time of my reservation but we had a drink at the bar and only waited a short while. Any restaurant setting its sights high has got to offer a combination of good food, ambience and service. When you experience really good service, it is incredible and a real delight. Poor service, on the other hand, can really affect the whole experience. A very grand impression was made from the moment I walked into the dining room. The number of options on the menu was small but interesting and they sourced most of the produce from either local farms or nearby towns. I asked a couple of questions about the food and got a completely blank response from our first waitress. The second didn't fare much better. It was clear that neither member of staff had any idea about the menu at all and hadn't been briefed by the chef. We made our somewhat uninformed selections and waited but a catalogue of poor service followed. The waitresses cleared tables noisily and dropped cutlery: it could have woken the dead! The starter came before the wine, there was more banging and crashing and people all around were waiting for their bills or condiments. It was complete chaos. The service was completely at odds to the experience the place was trying to provide. It charged big city prices without the equivalent service and I felt somehow cheated by the end of the evening. The poor service had turned a potentially fantastic evening into a damp squib. The next night we dined across the road in much more modest surroundings.

Ideas Can Come From Almost Anywhere

You don't have to be sitting in front of a desk to start a business. Sara Murray was waiting in a supermarket checkout when she temporarily lost her daughter. She was soon reunited but that feeling of complete helplessness got her thinking about a simple GPS device that could find a child, pet, old person, etc. almost instantly. She founded a company called 'Buddi' and started working on a prototype, got investor funding and launched her first product. In 2008, the business had a turnover in excess of £3m.

S tick to the Knitting

There is an old business school mantra that people should 'stick to the knitting', i.e. focus on one thing, do it well and not diversify into unfamiliar territory. As with many entrepreneurs who I have met over the years, I like diversity and relish the challenge of trying something new rather than sticking to the safety of what I already know.

Most really big firms are known for one thing; Cola-Cola, McDonald's, Microsoft, etc. have built great empires by applying their skills in a certain arena, scaling it up and trying to do things a little bit better each year. The people at the top are not limited in their thinking, but much more focused in their application. The lessons here are about understanding what works for you, what scope and framework are going to offer enough stimulation. There is absolutely no point in giving up the current job, starting something new and finding out in 12 months time (when the buzz and emotion has worn down a bit) that this actually isn't for you after all. In terms of diversity, Virgin is unlike virtually all other businesses because it deliberately looks to operate and move in to very different arenas. The reason it has been successful in most of the time is the understanding of its core skill. Virgin is not concerned with the business sector of industry, but on quality of delivery. What ties all their ventures together is the challenge of improving the delivery of service above the perceived norm. The key thing for all of us is to understand where we want to focus and be less concerned about the specific application.

Diversification

If you are curious about other sectors or like the idea of diversifying, there are some good rules that I have gained from working with great entrepreneurs.

* Gap – is the area you like the look of already an existing niche exploited by others or a new gap that has opened up. This should affect how you move into this space.

* New income – moving into areas can generate additional revenue streams but make sure it doesn't have a negative impact on your

mainstream business.

* Stay close – if you are in any doubt, try to look at opportunities close to your existing core skill or offering. It is likely that your experience and understanding will stand you in good stead. This is usually a good place to cut your teeth.

* Existing customers – can you sell anything new to the people you already have a good relationship with? What else might those companies or individuals want or need?

* Existing products – can you find new customers for your existing products or services? This might mean new marketing and/or promotional campaigns in different places or adding to the salesforce. I am a great believer in finding other individuals or companies that may want to sell your goods for a percentage. Look for people or organisations that don't have to increase their costs but might want to have an extra revenue stream themselves.

Outside Help – The Government

OI recently read a government budget statement outlining a primary aim to help small businesses. I went through the whole lot, line by line and couldn't find a single benefit for any of my companies or ventures. Not a solitary one! I did find some additional paperwork relating to a tax change and some other bits of new legislation that might have an impact when employing a bunch of graduates. Just what I need to help my businesses grow! In reality, my expectations were too high as I saw 'we will help you' and actually thought there might be something positive for me. I should have known better. I have known and had dealings with many politicians over the years but few have any experience of running their own small business. Let me give you an example; one of the first things we need to do if we have an idea and want to expand slightly is get some additional help in the shape of a new person. The amount of paperwork needed for what should be a simple procedure is crazy. The calculations required to pay a salary are incredible and include employees and employers National Insurance Contributions, tax rates, benefits I must offer and so on. I just don't understand why, given that small companies are supposed to be the lifeblood of any economy, employing people isn't easier. Every minute that we spend filling out all these forms and getting accountants to estimate employee costs, is time and money lost.

I set up a small, niche online business targeted at Chinese and Korean companies and wealthy individuals who want to come over to UK to play golf. For several decades, a constant stream of Japanese and Americans have been lured to these windswept shores to play golf and as a result have provided a great income for many. I wanted to replicate this for the Chinese and Korean markets so I spoke to a couple of UK government departments whose sole purpose it was to encourage trade and the best they could offer was an organised trip to China that I had to pay for. And it was expensive! Great Britain, as an example, doesn't have a huge bank of natural resources on its tourism balance sheet (the weather for a start) but it does have a few reasons why people would want to visit yet the government effort is far too generic. I saw some advertising trying to encourage Americans to come to the UK and couldn't believe the strategy.

Most people like to go to places for very specific reasons so targeting those desires will increase tourist numbers: in my opinion a picture of The Tower of London with a bland message about how old it is definitely won't. This is really about looking differently at the assets of the country and identifying how to create and increase revenue streams from them. As my example illustrates, there are plenty of golfers from all over the globe who would come to our world-renowned courses, if it were easier to arrange and coordinate. We need our government to think as differently as our entrepreneurs and business people. What a missed opportunity. Sorry – rant over!

Outside Help – Consultancies

Market research, strategy, technical and other external consultants can be very helpful when branching out on your own or looking to evaluate a new opportunity. In my experience, they can give a lot of credibility to possible courses of action, often to the likes of banks but also to possible business partners or investors. What I soon found out, however, about using outside consultants is that they usually have very different objectives to ourselves. They are trying to portray the information they dig up or pull together in a saleable and reusable manner, not increase the scope of a business. In other words, they are mostly concerned with the 'cosmetics' of a business, and not with its successful operation. I have found that taking some time to talk to companies up and down your particular business value chain and asking for their assessment of how things could improve is often a far more successful (and cheaper) option.

Business Comfort Zone

Why is it that so many good ideas fail to move forward or come to full fruition? I've seen so many ordinary concepts succeed and lots of clever ones languish because people have taken different approaches. This often has to do with our comfort zone in business. Developing into a new workspace requires a desire to see what is outside the area of reassurance and calm. I always had a fear in the back of my mind of being ripped off because I didn't know the ropes or the way other businesses worked. It made me cautious but I tried to turn that on its head through a combination of playing stupid and not accepting the way others did things as necessarily the right way. Many elements define our comfort zone such as natural instincts, behaviour, experience, skillset and timing, but if there is one way to expand our horizons: improve the way we deal with people. Making sure others are on our wavelength, getting them to appreciate our honesty and integrity, will stand us in good stead. A willingness to keep pushing back the boundaries is one of the strongest themes running through the successful people I have met. These themes are expressed in different ways, but it is about reaching a place where we enjoy the new challenges that our careers throw at us.

Selling

When starting my first business, I was often presenting in front of different individuals and groups of potential clients, trying to persuade them to come on-board. I had always thought there were good, natural sales-types and then the rest of us, and that selling was a numbers game of knocking on lots of doors. The more I knocked, the more I became intrigued by the relationship that was formed, sometimes in just a few minutes. A bond of trust needed to be established between two people built usually on mutual respect, understanding and a few ground rules.

One of the key things for me was getting my behaviour right, in particular, moderating my 'lets go' nature, with the ability to listen and really empathise with those around me. The temptation to promise the earth was great but I managed to resist, most of the time at least, learning that a bond developed early on in a business relationship always needs attention. If a mistake has been made or promise not kept, I needed to act swiftly to remedy the situation. All of my early clients were different in the service they expected but had the same need to be kept informed. They had bosses, business partners, fellow directors, team members and other departments who needed to know when work was going to be delivered. Any movement in schedules could affect many others and this could impact on the people I dealt with. I also soon learnt that delivering a product or service to a client a day early might earn respect but being a day late can be regarded as failure and undo lots of good work at a stroke.

'You can accomplish anything in life, provided that you do not mind who gets the credit.' Harry Truman

Partnerships

Did you know that Starbucks, McDonald's, Hyatt Hotels and many supermarket and pizza chains round the globe have built their business on the idea of franchising? It can be very rewarding for both sides, especially when local people are helped by a larger company bringing economies of scale and knowledge of customer behaviour into play. The concept of franchising can be applied to many other commercial areas and it is a useful exercise to look at the model underpinning the business. It is about outsourcing activities in a controlled manner to people who are highly incentivised to succeed. This kind of application could leave us with time to focus on other priorities whilst keeping different parts of the business life growing profitably. This may also lead to the possibility of out-sourcing part, or all, of your own role, potentially providing greater flexibility.

Rewarding Loyalty

My local Costa coffee shop gave me a loyalty card recently. The deal was to make ten purchases and get the next one free. I usually can't be bothered with these sorts of schemes as I either lose the coupon or end up carrying a whole wallet full of meaningless bits of paper. A medicinal decaf every now and again, however, could do no harm so I started getting the small card stamped. I got to eight stamps before finding myself in a different Costa buying a warming brew. I paid and showed the ticket to the attractive girl behind the counter who looked at me with some amusement. She asked what the ticket was as if I was asking her to fill in a lottery form. I explained but she had never heard of the scheme. I was disgruntled as the prize of that free cup was no closer. The following day I found myself waiting for a train and spotted another Costa. I went through the ordering

> 'When you're the first person whose beliefs are different from what everyone else believes, you're basically saying, 'I'm right and everyone else is wrong'. That's a very unpleasant position to be in. It's at once exhilarating and at the same time an invitation to be attacked'. Larry Ellison, Founder of Oracle

process and again showed my slightly more worn loyalty ticket. The guy said the stamper had been lost so he couldn't help me. I was definitely not encouraged to be a regular user. I now take a slightly longer route to the office (more exercise has got to be better for me) and get my hit from Starbucks instead.

Personal Profile – Mark

Background – a qualified architect and partner in a medium-sized London-based practice. He believes his profession has had a major influence on his outlook and how he approaches all aspects of life. After a less than glorious initial educational experience, he found a desire to go into architecture, attracted by the mix of creative and discipline. He enjoyed the seven years of training and getting established in business after qualifying, but also believes in the thorough and exacting standards that building large structures requires.

Success – his profession has helped to deconstruct problems by applying his technical skills but one of the biggest challenges in the progress of his career was managing people. This was something that was a glaring omission from his education. Success for him was not only acquiring more practical knowledge but also learning how to bring the best out of people and managing the expectations of those in his business group. He had one junior employee who he realised, after several months of toiling, would need his help, if he was to progress. He therefore had to place some of his own priorities on hold, while helping someone else. This ended up being a very liberating experience and the project was completed successfully. When made a full partner, he became aware that as an equity holder, a large part of the success of the business was in other people's hands, so he had to broaden his aims and objectives. Architect practices in recessions are usually hard hit and Mark is under no illusions that corporate success in tough times is about keeping the doors open. He has helped the business develop new clients, thereby reducing the reliance on a few and this is something he has found very fulfilling.

Work Balance – part of Mark's balance is found in feeling able to do his job well but also in having enough left in the tank to engage with his wife and family. This isn't just spending time with them, but sharing their activities and connecting with each of them as individuals. Just being around, simply isn't enough.

Retirement – is something he hasn't given a great deal of thought to and would ideally like a sabbatical at some point over the next ten years, to spend some quality time with his family. This would give him the opportunity to identify what the next chapter might contain. He still enjoys the application of his technical skills and the challenge of designing original buildings, something that is always evolving due to social attitudes, new materials and government regulations. His father was also an architect and enjoyed working freelance well after the statutory retirement date. One step towards retiring would certainly be moving to three or four days in the office per week and the remainder at home. His profession hasn't been very quick at grasping flexible working practices but he feels it's something that could have a significant influence in future. Mark understands the need for all areas of the architectural process to come together quite regularly to bounce ideas and communicate different views therefore accepting too much flexibility could have adverse results. Ultimately better buildings get made when all disciplines communicate well.

Advice – starting his own business seems scary but is an aspiration. The overriding piece of advice is to spend enough time to work out what we are striving for in life and what we really want to get out of it. Once we know this, the future has a great deal more clarity and purpose.

Financing Good Ideas

The most frequent reason people give for not developing something new is lack of finance. There are many ways of looking at funding requrements and most of the successful people I have met look more creatively at how to raise money. The first stage in financing any venture or new product is to know how much cash you need. It sounds easy but it's raely a simple calculation. The amount required to develop a commercial idea and bring it to a saleable or marketable state is often not the moment when the bank balance will be at its lowest ebb. Identifying the peak borrowing requirement is about finding that time when income outweighs outgoings on a permanent basis, when all running costs are taken into account.

I set up a small creative services company many years ago with a couple of good young people; they were very talented in their field but didn't have much business experience. I asked them about the money that we would need and they didn't really know where to start. We chatted about the usual sorts of costs like salaries, rent, equipment, etc. and arrived at a figure, which they seemed happy with. The business wasn't exactly starting from a zero base as we had a number of clients ready to go, but it would take three or four months at least before we were operating fully. I then estimated the average credit period during the first year would be at least 60 days. Getting establish on customer databases, opening accounts, issuing invoices at the end of the process and getting them to the right person, all takes time. I anticipated it would be over a year before we hit the maximum indebtedness, but it sent my colleagues into a bit of a spin. The fact that we would work hard for a whole year and have very little in the bank seemed crazy to them, when we were doing everything possible to keep upfront costs down. I welcomed them to the world of business!

Raising Cash

I was trying to raise some money for a large TV series some years ago and it was at a time when international co-financing and co-productions were in favour, so I was not expecting it to be too difficult. I realised that we needed to show potential production partners, i.e. television and media companies in other parts of the world, especially America, Australia, South Africa and the Far East, we were serious and could deliver the project properly. At the same time, it was vital for us to retain the overall ownership if we were to profit fully from the upside. I saw a number of UK-based finance partners but it was too small for them and they really wanted security from the assets of the entire company. No-one wanted to be first to invest and the talk was about seeing our track record for a few years to make sure we were as solid as I was saying. This taught me the first lesson in finance: start your dialogue and relationships when you don't need cash, then they will be much more receptive when you do.

By being in the right place at the right time, I managed to help acquire the rights to produce three cooking/travel series with a British *bon vivre* chef. He had a long-running relationship with the BBC but both wanted a different kind of deal. Like many entertainment personalities, this larger than life guy could have his moments and it was at a time when the BBC wanted to produce less of their own material. I had a good meeting with BBC executives, who still liked the idea of the series, but were concerned about whether we could finance the project. Taking such a well-known personality and a big crew to a far off country for seven or eight weeks plus post-production, research, etc. would not come cheap. The BBC didn't want to put this in their schedule and then us not to deliver. They refused to sign any contract until I could prove to them that we could control the cashflow properly which meant showing how we would sell the rights to overseas broadcasters. The other option was to pre-sell overseas and other rights to increase confidence levels. I had some good relationships with several media and entertainment companies round the world and managed to sell the series to six broadcasters before we had started filming. I went back to the BBC and showed them the confirmation and finally they were happy. As soon as we had the BBC signed up, the remaining rights sold quickly. Without a few good relationships, I would probably still be peddling that show! The first series was widely acclaimed and had good audience figures, enabling us to produce two further series, all of which were financially successful.

Equity versus Debt

I have often been advised to make a three-year business plan, detailed cashflow forecasts and balance sheets when setting up my ventures. With hindsight, the first thing I needed to think about before putting pen to paper was how I felt about equity and debt. As a simple example, would I feel happier giving away part of the business or having the bank on my back? To this day, I find dealing with the beaurocracy of banking systems completely maddening. So many people saying, 'how can I help you' and so few of them actually being able to help at all. If I ever actually got to speak to a manager, they couldn't make any decisions and getting even the simplest things done took an age. We do need banks in order to do business but it is helpful to reduce our dependence on them as much as possible, as time spent chasing down bank employees is not productive. These tasks are definitely on the wrong side of our happiness spectrum! On the other hand, equity partners don't come without implications and issues to think hard about. The first issue to me, overriding absolutely everything else, is the alignment of objectives. It's possible for partnerships to work in different ways and move at different paces, but only when they are trying to reach the same end goal, is it likely to succeed.

I have always liked the concept of preference-type equity,

where someone takes a shareholding in a company or venture but also receives a guaranteed return (usually smaller than returns enjoyed by traditional venture capital but nonetheless a percentage yield). This is sometimes referred to as mezzanine finance as it sits neatly between equity and debt. The people running the business can't forget their equity partner and it is often a good discipline for the management to have a cost attached to the capital it is using. The coupon or percentage need not be huge but it does set a good precedent for all sides. When we purchase shares in big business, we can easily vote with our feet: just sell the shares and move on. In smaller companies or ventures, things don't work that way and our options may be limited to a long-term exit plan or some kind of restructuring. Offering this type of finance might just bring people to the table who would be otherwise reserved about participation.

Third Party Cash

A young guy came to me with a really good advertising delivery idea some years ago and seemed to have done a lot of research into how it would work. He had a good understanding of the dynamics of the business and felt the concept was quite scalable. His commercial experience, at that time, was working for a couple of big companies and therefore he wasn't sure how the fundamentals of the start-up company would work. Importantly he didn't place much value on them. We met and discussed the numbers and how he would run the business until I asked him what he was putting in. I explained he needed to show commitment to the project (and myself) in a financial sense. He wasn't prepared to compromise on his earnings, depending on the performance of the business, and failed to see why he should forgo an additional chunk of the equity, if things didn't go according to his plan. From my perspective, this late-twenty-something guy wanted others to take all the risk and didn't want to compromise any of the downside. Rather predictably, the venture never got off the ground and to this day, the chap continues to work for big companies. For myself, along with many others like me, it's not about how much people actually have to invest, it's more about attitude. I think this defines the very nature of the entrepreneur and the sort of workplace relationship we each should be looking for.

Amount of Debt versus Scope of Venture

I am a great believer in looking at ways to start things on a small scale. Few ventures I have been involved in have ended up exactly the same concept as they originated. The amazing revolution in IT and the Internet has changed the entire fundamentals of many companies, even if they are selling a similar product or service to the same group of customers. There are ways to ensure that growth is not restricted or overly costly, especially when it comes to how trade suppliers and potential partners are tied to the venture.

This is about thinking big and acting small. I was approached by a person with a good e-commerce idea, but he was struggling with how to move it forward. It was a niche e-tailer concept and made good use of his experience of nearly 20 years. He had a small number of suppliers already signed up but needed a great-looking website, so he could attract more clients and start building online traffic. He didn't have a huge budget at the start but needed the site to look professional and polished. I had worked with him for many years and, whilst having great energy, he could become distracted by the potential of new ideas and not fully exploit existing assets. I proposed a deal to him to build and maintain the site plus handle his e-marketing and SEO (search engine optimisation) but he would have to guarantee a minimum number of new products each month. I would get a fee spread over the first year that would reduce his start-up outlay. I think this deal falls into that category where both sides have something to gain and lose. I was investing time and knowledge and he was forgoing other avenues.

It's not always possible to construct deals like this but it may be surprising what is possible. I have seen many suppliers and providers agree to a relationship which is well outside their normal terms of business. If we can persuade people or companies to be real partners in an idea, scheme or venture, it can be attractive from a number of perspectives. Many of us want to break out of our current business model but are just not sure how to do it. Once we have others on board, the added advantage is that new business opportunities could well develop as the network expands.

Angels on High

There are a surprisingly large number of people out there who might be willing to join with you to help grow or realise a life-changing idea. Take a look at angelsden.co.uk, a site that tries to match entrepreneurs needing finance with those that want to invest. Even if you don't decide this alternative is for you, it is well worth meeting some of these people to obtain feedback and see how they operate. This might just be of use further down the road.

> **'Smart money is the best – it's about connecting people who have good ideas with others who actively want to invest some cash and also want to be involved.'**

Letting Go

A topic that kept coming up as I researched this book was delegation: that art of letting go of what seems important at the time and avoiding the temptation to micro-manage. There are a couple of big issues here and the first is about getting into a state of mind where we feel comfortable to hand over responsibility to others without worrying about the consequences. It's not that we don't care about the result or impact, it's learning to acccept that we can't do everything ourselves. We somehow need to be looking forward to that feeling of watching others benefit from also being fully engaged. There has been little in my career that has given me more pleasure than watching people improve their skills, grow in confidence and see new areas of business as great opportunities. Without that mix of experience and confidence they would have stood still. Delegation has also enabled me to explore many new commercial avenues, build a strong network and have greater work–life balance at the same time.

Analysis versus Instinct

It is possible to over-analyse opportunities, deals and ventures that hit our desk on a daily basis. Most entrepreneurs I have met rely considerably on their instinct and try not to get too bogged down in the detail before making a big decision. Once the direction has been set, it's then about looking at the nuts-and-bolts to make sure the execution is good. The key for all of us is to understand what sort of decision-maker we are and how much research, data and general information we need to feel comfortable. I tend to be more intuitive and instinctive in areas where I have a better grasp of the basics. I am certaionly less instinctive, when I can't get a handle on the value chain (i.e. who gets what share of the pie) or core principles. I naturally like doing things differently but just don't want to look like a complete fool (too often!).

As part of my degree course, I spent a very enlightening year working at the European head office of American Express. They took their research and development function very seriously as understanding cardholder habits, needs and desires was absolutely crucial for them. After all, this was a credit card you had to pay off at the end of the each month and had, at that time, to pay an annual fee to have one, while their competitors were free. It was accepted at fewer places than its major rivals and given a choice most shops and restaurants would prefer we used something else. Looking at what cardholders would really value was therefore crucial in the fight to keep and grow their share of the market. They were continually looking to maintain their upmarket positioning, but many people still wanted something more than pure ostentation. Research carried out compared whether this was travel insurance or a wine club, exclusive travel offers or tickets to special events. Analysing demographics and spending patterns was one thing but really understanding the lifestyles and aspirations of existing and potential cardholders was key to their future. This was not the sort of business that could rely on gut feel alone but something I always felt was missing from the research process was how to establish the company as innovative and forward thinking in the minds of its cardholders. For me, this was about offering things that were really different and imaginative that we wouldn't expect from a credit card company, thereby seeding in people's minds the thought that having this piece of plastic may bring intangible benefits.

Fortune Favours the Brave

I grew up watching a lot of war and cowboy films, seeing heroes do remarkably brave deeds and riding off into the sunset with the girl as the credits roll. When I went into business, it always seemed to be that the first cowboy down the canyon, usually got a arrow in his back. How could this be? I thought that courage would be rewarded properly and had to quickly learn that making a success with new or pioneering ventures needs more than just a good idea. It requires meticulous planning, an eye for detail, good timing and a good deal of luck. Most of the business school books I read downplay the role of luck, probably because the element of chance underplays the disciplines they are trying to teach. There aren't many successful people I have met, however, who can't say that at times lady luck hasn't been shining on them. This doesn't mean we should treat our careers and business lives like a game of roulette, more that we should be aware we can succeed when we may not deserve to, and vice versa. If we do benefit from a bit of good fortune, my advice is to make the most of it, as things might be different next time. If we have thought things through from all angles and been diligent in our approach to key tasks, we are giving ourselves every chance to succeed. This is all most entrepreneurs want.

Attitude to Risk

We are all different when it comes to investing time, money, effort and our reputation in new projects or business ventures. Our default position tends to be either natural caution or over-optimism, based on the situation we are in and a host of other personal factors. I have seen many people who are not initially excited about a proposition get swept along on the back of a wave of prospective activity – the sheer anticipation of something new or the brilliant people around them. In research and discussions, I have seen five primary factors affecting how we respond:
1) Experience – if we have seen similar things before, we often move more quickly.

2) Knowledge – most of us are more likely to take a risk in an area we know something about.

3) Gut feel – many of us still rely (often for very good reasons) on our initial instinct.

4) Desire – we want to be part of something because of the potential rewards including financial, reputation, lifestyle, etc.

5) Current situation – if we are unhappy with our status quo, we are more likely to try something new.

The key to this analysis is to get a better understanding of our attitude to risk and what factors affect our levels of caution or optimism at any point in time. Many of us get involved with projects or ideas when relationships with partners, friends or work colleagues are going well. We feel bullish and confident and can forget to review the downsides in our usual manner. This is exactly the time to pause for thought.

'Sir Martin (Sorrell) has never made any pretence of the fact that he lives for his business and has no separation of his business and personal lives. As with all pure entrepreneurs, WPP is his life. 'The three circles that matter are family, career and society,' he says, 'There are very few people that manage to balance it. I certainly haven't been able to. You could probably balance two, but balancing all three is phenomenally difficult.' from *The Secrets of CEOs* by Steve Tappin and Andrew Cave

Process Re-design

Sometimes the best way forward is to take a step back. To rethink and review your business process could mean looking at how you interface with other companies, how your workflow is operating and what routines make up the full picture of your activities. Most businesses are not designed at a single point in time they evolve and change as time passes, often in strange and unusual ways. Different personnel will always have an effect as individuals naturally alter processes to best fit their own skills or requirements. This all leads to a picture of businesses that are operating in far from the most efficient or helpful manner for all concerned. One issue relating to any re-design concept is that some people will be pro and others against, reflecting insecurities or concerns about how change could affect their position. Any process of re-evaluation needs to start by trying to get everyone on board, making sure all negative comments are aired and discussed. Once this is done, the process can throw up some useful ideas for restructuring or implementing. Starting with a blank sheet of paper, try to visualise your business process by linking the various elements and interconnections. On a separate page, map out what might be an ideal or much simpler flow of events. This exercise will create a value chain from one end of your activities to the other.

Control and Outsourcing

Outsourcing can improve flexibility and efficiency in every business, but the issue of where it should start and end is a very real one. The generally conceived wisdom is that we should retain ownership of core and strategic areas, but I tend to think it's actually about what tasks we perform better than others. If another individual or company prove cheaper, quicker, slicker, more technically advanced, more creative, or simply offer a better service, it may be that using their strength can help your business. The key is in the deal. If you are a small firm with a large outsource partner, you won't have much leverage, but there are usually ways of working so that everyone is happy in the long term. One note of caution: I have seen a couple of businesses sign very good outsourcing deals, but who have subsequently moved into a comfort zone and now act as if they don't need to keep evolving, changing or developing. Both have weakened their operations by relying on other companies and have not seen the need to push back the boundaries of product development, service levels, marketing support, product enhancements, online marketing or other differentiating elements.

The Spare Room

Can you start a business from your spare room, garage or even garden shed, for that matter? Why not? Many benefits can be found from a low-cost and fast start. Your idea for a business doesn't have to be a huge or expansive concept from the outset, just a small gap in the market, something you can do better than others whether it be an international product or simple local service. When turning a home space into a work area, however, the lifestyle balance is even more important and it's best to get it right from the start. Even though you'll be working domestically there should be a strong sense of keeping office and home separate, making sure you have a space to be creative, businesslike, run your technology with ease and switch off when you need to. Many people have under-invested in their home office, installing mediocre software on a slow computer, have a noisy printer and don't have enough bandwidth. This is all about being able to function smoothly and compete with other, often large or well-funded companies, on a proper footing and certainly not at a noticeable disadvantage from the outset. Your technology can't slow things down, be inferior or your service will be. What is needed is a fast computer with plenty of hard-drive space, a good ISP and band-width for all eventualities, latest versions of software and often extras such as a webcam, VOIP (Voice Over Internet – such as Skype) and an audio recorder. These can really pay off, when talking to new clients. One of the other big failings I have seen is website design. So many small companies and individuals try to do this on the cheap, getting it created by the 15-year-old son of the next door neighbour or worse. We don't all need to learn how to use Flash, html coding or Dreamweaver, but we do have to under-stand the importance of a good website as a marketing and branding tool, as well as the basis of website thinking, including how users will move around a site, purchase, respond and react. I cover online thinking in more detail in chapter 8.

Emma Jones, wrote a book entitled, *Spare Room Start Up* and in it states, 'After five years of working for a multinational corporation, in a job that took me all over the world, I decided to come home. I was 27. And I wanted, more than anything, to be my own boss, to start my own business and to take control of my lifestyle. So I cleared out the spare room, invested in a new laptop and started to make calls. That was the beginning of Techlocate, an inward investment consultancy that grew to employing five people in home offices in London and Manchester. Two years after starting up, I successfully sold the business to the sort of corporation I'd left behind.'

Personal Profile – John

Background – he joined the family chemical business straight from school and had to work his way up through the company, doing every job along the way, ending up as chairman. He is a highly motivated person who is as happy discussing issues over a pint of beer with delivery drivers, as he is presenting strategy to his fellow directors. He is a natural entrepreneur and has taken his business interests further and broader than most could ever imagine.

Success – John states, 'most people who work for themselves work very hard to start with, the clever ones get people to work hard for them and then slow down. The real chargers keep working hard and build empires or go bust because they extend themselves in some way. Ever since the world began there have been entrepreneurs, they take risk, work hard and enjoy the fruits of their labours. Hannibal, Sir Walter Raleigh; go through your history books and make a list of the old boys who gave it a go. Different times result in different achievements for these people. In the 1800,s, they would have travelled the world and now they are self-employed businessmen and women. Many of them are unemployable.'

Work Balance – he loves the cut and thrust of business life, the interaction with different people and thinks many entrepreneurs he has met would have been pirates a couple of hundred years ago. Technology has made most of us work harder and longer, labouring away on trains, in cars, on planes and just about anywhere we can perch for a length of time. Many, he believes, seem to enjoy the pace or certainly can't seem to live without it. Everyone has their own special ways of dealing with stress but John has the ability to switch off for an hour or two, rest up and then come back to the problem or issue. Success happens when we feel really happy with the decisions you have made. But he, like many other entrepreneurs, will still strive to try to improve on those decisions next time around.

Retirement – John outlines, 'retirement is not a pipe dream! It's an awful thought, meaning you are no longer good enough to compete in this wicked world. If retirement means challenging yourself in another direction, then fine. But don't retire. I actually enjoy working so why should I stop doing something I enjoy and am good at? If you are spending all your time thinking about retirement, then the chances are you are not a natural entrepreneur'.

Advice – he feels we should, 'never worry, as a problem is just a good decision waiting to be made. People who have chosen to work for themselves usually set their own goals, set their own targets in life, choose how hard to work and take risks along the way and then decide when they want to do something different. Most will not retire in a traditional sense or in the same way as someone who has always been an employee. I would compare the movers and shakers through history with us today. We are able to do so much more because of technology. Modern success is instant'.

Business Opportunities

Sometimes the process of pitching for new business can be rewarding and helpful in itself, especially when trying to get our heads around other companies perspectives and business models. One of the growing trends in business and one that has been identified by many of the people interviewed, is continuity. With better communications and information at our fingertips, we are more inclined to try a different supplier or strike a deal with a new business partner, something that can now be completed very quickly. The days of being able to rely on long-standing commercial relationships for future prosperity, is at an end. Any person who thinks they cannot lose clients or a potentially critical proportion of their turnover, is away with the fairies. In order to keep developing and growing, therefore, we all need to think about winning new business. For one of my companies that operates in quite a volatile environment, I estimated losing 10-

15% of business each year, which means it has to find 20% more per annum just to make marginal progress.

Managing Expectations

It's not always easy to judge how much better we are going to feel about ourselves or whether we have any more money in our pocket as a result of a better work experience. I have certainly been in a number of jobs when good results have been achieved and little recognition or reward has been forthcoming. It's easy to get frustrated but in the long run what we get out is definitely related to what we put in. Whilst working for MGM, I was really keen to move one particular aspect of the operation forward by using the established distribution strength of a third party. After much corporate soul-searching, we signed a deal with the entertainment software giant, Electronic Arts to develop and market a range of new interactive games using the James Bond license and other film franchises. I worked on the negotiations for months, which went back and forth, looking at how intellectual properties might be exploited, royalty rates, timing of releases and who would have final creative say. It was one of those classic situations when the companies wanted to do a deal, but came from different industries and didn't really understand the other. I was truly ecstatic when we finally completed the contract and was waiting for the roar of applause from across the pond, the champagne to flow and a lavish amount of praise. By this time though, the bosses seemed to have moved on to something else and didn't appear to see the significance of the deal. After a few discrete inquiries and some closed-door calls, I learnt that because the deal wouldn't have any great impact on the current year earnings, it was viewed as something that might be valuable as opposed to a relationship of great immediate importance. I could only see that combining MGM's library of intellectual property rights with Electronic Arts talent at developing great computer games and global distribution, was going to produce something special. I learned the lesson that until the money starts flowing, no-one should expect to see champagne corks flying through the air.

Looking for Trends

Looking for Trends

Good ideas can come in any sector or area of business but ones which piggy-back growing markets and customer trends often have a greater chance of success. This is not just because in an expanding sector there can be better margins, it's also more likely that the big boys haven't spotted the gaps or haven't move fast enough to take full advantage. Any industry that is growing and evolving throws up opportunities for those who are quick on their feet and looking in a fresh way. I have listed some trends that might be of interest below:

* Climate change – this is beginning to affect individuals, but will increasingly influence companies as well.

* Health – in most developed economies, the population is getting older and there will be a greater demand for products and services for older or retired people.

* Migrations – it is easier to travel and move anywhere in the world than ever before. We have seen unprecedented numbers of European workers coming to the UK to earn a living and improve their language skills. These sorts of movements are not going away as it becomes ever-easier to find out about what other places offer and even quicker to get there.

* Education – the need for education or re-training of both young-sters and adults has never been greater. Whether it is learning the basics of literacy and numeracy or retraining skills, technology or other disciplines, there will always be a need over and above what any government currently provides.

* Local – many people are seeing the benefit to their community of buying local produce or sourcing local services. For many consumers there is a greater value in something that doesn't have lots of airmiles or any at all.

Final Thoughts – Brave New World

Improving our work experience, by starting a venture or exploring a commercial idea, should be a major goal for all of us. This is not just to say that we have given something a go, but for the experience of something new. Analysing opportunities should be done, however, after we have looked at exactly what we want and where we would ultimately like to be in our career. Some of the other things raised in this chapter are as follows:

– Service – we are now living through a service revolution and providing better help and assistance can have a powerful influence on buyer behaviour.

– Starting a business – can look daunting at first sight but the only way to really test the water is to jump in. There will be lots of people giving advice but none of them wear your shoes. Find the things you are really good at and get people to help with the other elements. The time to get started is as soon as you are able, waiting rarely improves anything as the benefits from the learning curve are very real.

– Outside help – don't expect too much from outside consultancies and agencies, especially when those companies or organisations have very differing objectives.

– Selling – is about forming a unique bond of trust and understanding.

– Money – if you need to raise finance, look at all the alternatives including trade sources, colleagues, business partners and others who might benefit from your success.

– Risk – identify your attitude to risk and monitor how this changes over time and different commercial circumstances.

– Work in parallel – getting something moving doesn't mean you have to resign or start thinking about your leaving party: it's worth getting your project to a state where it can provide good revenue. In the short term, look to get other trusted people to help build momentum and if you have to give a percentage of your business away, that is far better than having 100% of nothing.

Random Mind Matter

* 'The word "innovation" conjures up the image of a process that is spontaneous, unpredictable, and unmanageable. Innovation literature abounds with stories of serendipitous discoveries and independent-minded champions doggedly pursuing an idea until they hit the jackpot. Often – as the stories stress – inventors worked in secret against the will of management.' Jeremy Kourdi, *100 Great Business Ideas*.

* Clear vision – if you don't have a clear idea or vision of what job or role you actually want to be doing, join the club with the

vast majority of us. However, given time our career mission does begin to emerge, but you have to be open to your feelings and search hard.

* Career success – to be successful in a chosen career is usually a lot easier if we have a good social life. It sounds basic but the higher up we go in the workplace, the more difficult it is to have a rounded and fulfilling life outside work. Some social activities which are useful to our personal development, relationships, friends and family inevitably end up getting dropped.

* Honesty is the best policy – it's amazing what brutal, no-holds-barred honesty can bring. Often others respond really positively even though the news is sometimes really bad for them. If Bill Clinton had given us the full story rather than saying something like 'I did not have sexual relations with that woman', things might have been a whole lot easier for him and his family.

* Shares fair – stock options have traditionally been a great way of getting bosses and senior staff to stay around. A small web investment company called On-Line PLC, was one such business who did this although when its share price (like just almost everyone else's during 2008) nose-dived, they needed to re-think. Share options were, at best, a gamble for employees and, at worst, an annoyance. When share prices fall so badly, schemes like this can be completely counter-productive. The company wanted to retain key staff and keep them motivated so decided to turn to an incentive scheme, which reduced the share price level far below prices previously agreed. This has all sorts of problems, not least how it equates to shareholder returns, given that they have already lost a considerable proportion of their investment. This is a classic situation of a company that is only thinking in a single direction. Rather than giving financial incentives, which may or may not motivate, they could be developing a much more lasting bond with their senior people using lifestyle and non-financial rewards. It they were to chat to each of the key personnel involved (and there were only five on the previous stock option scheme) and try to persuade them to look at non-financial rewards, it might just help everyone out of this problem of evaluation by money alone. Why not change the job and working environment to fit in with the person involved!

6 Mind, Body and Business

Aim

Being out of balance in life can have a big impact on our mind, body and just about every part of our behaviour. In this chapter we examine how others have tackled this problem and focus on the impact of our senses, outlook and attitudes on our overall well-being and happiness.

'Success is 80% about having the right mindset and 20% about the right skills.'
Nicola Cook, *A New You*

Limited Resources

For an alarmingly large proportion of us, exhaustion, stress, tension, anxiety and even forms of depression have become an inescapable part of life. This is a shocking failure of our ability to create a work–life culture that can maintain our well-being, rather than simply eat away at it. A job which requires too great a proportion of our time, energy, plus emotional and physical resources is one which is not be sustainable in the long term. The impact and cost is felt, not just by ourself, but by everyone around us. I have interviewed many entrepreneurs with the vast majority seeming to have a really strong understanding of the relationship between their mind and body. This results in them making better decisions about their levels of self-confidence and spotting the signs before something bad happens. Acting like a successful person is more than simply buying a smart outfit, it's about realising the connection between our thoughts and actions.

The situation we face is made more difficult because of the emotionally draining impact many careers now require. Working too hard results in longer hours spent not just in the office, but thinking about work as well or taking calls, texts and emails. As a result, we have less time available to do things that strengthen our resolve and make us happy and balanced. We have only to look at the statistics on the number of days lost to sickness to see how our bodies and minds are becoming weighed down. This is

Whether we like it or not, we do not have a limitless bank of human resources. No matter how fit or positive we are, the impact of the over-work culture will lead to a deterioration in our ability to fight illness, and will reduce our natural levels of self-confidence, self-assurance and self-esteem.

something that a two-week holiday in the sun will not cure. Admittedly, it would do no great harm either!

'Great spirits have always encountered violent opposition from mediocre minds. The mediocre mind is incapable of understanding the man who refuses to bow blindly to conventional prejudices and chooses instead to express his opinions courageously and honestly.' Albert Einstein

Arm's Length Relationships

I met up recently with a guy from school days, who is a partner in an architect company, is married and has several kids. He reminded me of the carefree existence we once had and the good times we spent together as a group of teenagers. He outlined that most of his relationships are now conducted via email or text rather than face-to-face. Even when he did get together with friends, it usually seemed to be for a quick meal as he was always rushing to do something else. It was as if the importance we once placed on proper human interaction had diminished in order to allow for a whole raft of new things, work-related stuff being a large part. While we might reward ourselves after a endless meetings with a trip to the gym or shops, this reward culture itself reduces the time we actually have left to be with friends, in a relaxed environment. Just sitting, chatting, being ourselves, laughing with each other and generally being gregariously human seems to have gone out of fashion. It's a basic instinct that we seem to have lost the taste for and I believe we actually need more now than at any stage in our evolution.

The comparison with the environment around us is very pertinent and appropriate as the parallels are strangely fitting. We have placed so little value on ourselves and the world around us, that we have managed to devalue them both. We have put other needs ahead of our really basic ones. Working too hard means we have lost the ability to make good decisions about how to spend our time. We had a really tough week at work so we go and buy a new and much improved washing machine or dishwasher, laptop computer or leather sofa. Any of these will have an immediate feeling of reward but will last for only a short while. These things often do very little to help the natural world around us and usually quite the opposite.

We Need to Invest

I have been looking at putting a wood burner in my home. A small token gesture in global ecological terms, but none the less a step in the right direction. I went to the local supermarket and petrol station to price packs of wood, etc. and was horrified at the cost. I was walking in the countryside nearby and saw a pile of logs which had clearly been cut down some time ago but hadn't been used for anything. Their only purpose seemed to be to partially block the footpath where walkers liked to ramble. In half a dozen visits to similarly shady places, I found trees that had been cut and left to rot every time. What a waste! I did some research and found that when (most) trees are cut down, they need a good period (minimum of a year for harder wood) of drying if they are to be used for fires inside the house. I wanted to find out if anyone could just go and pick up wood left around and called the local authority. The response was quite funny, if it wasn't typically apathetic. The lady I spoke to wasn't sure, but would get back to me. She didn't call back so I picked up the phone again and eventually got a statement about how they were trying not to encourage people to go round picking up wood that was lying around. So, one of our basic instincts as humans (to forage) and something that was actually good for the environment (i.e. utilising wood that would otherwise be of little or no value to society) rather than using electricity or gas, was not encouraged. Many find comfort in the *status quo* which can make the progress of change more complicated and difficult.

Personal Profile – Jim

Background – his education was very much science-focused and completed an engineering degree with top marks. Now managing director of a successful international family business employing around 100 people across a number of sites in the UK.

Success – Jim believes success is the achievement of our own goals and that many of us get distracted into striving for others' needs and wants. There seems to be greater pressure than ever to be more aspirational and to strive for goals, which have less meaning to us as individuals. We need to re-focus, somehow, on the journey rather than simply the destination. A spiritual person, for example, has the simple goal of imparting knowledge and wisdom to others and reaches enlightenment with the success of others rather than himself. When we are so preoccupied with the end result, we often don't see the beauty in things along the way.

Work Balance – the early part of his life was more driven by negative feelings such as the fear of failure or letting down others, than by the achievement of his own goals. He has now turned this around and strives to look at the joy, pleasure and excitement to be found both in his job and outside of working. He gets a huge amount of satisfaction from helping others to achieve things and is a Prince's Trust mentor. His work focus and constant aim is maintaining the quality of the end product and getting everyone to appreciate the importance of dealing with customers, suppliers and internal staff. He feels if we try to enjoy the connection with people, we will be better at what we do and also happier.

Retirement – the ultimate work goal is to make himself redundant, so the business can run without him. Jim outlines that there have traditionally been three phases in our lives: learning, doing and, finally, not doing. This has now changed to learning, doing and less doing. We need to continue to search for stimulus and new challenges to keep us occupied and purposeful. This ensures we are happy as we feel more useful, content and valuable as individuals. As an example, learning something new is very important at whatever age. He recently started studying trees and now gets the benefit simply by going for a walk and understanding why certain species grow well in particular conditions. A little information has brought a lot of happiness to him.

Advice – we should act as a mentor for someone. Also often problems can be caused at work when other people restrict the flow of information and learning, usually because they are fearful or insecure about their own position. This affects many others up and down the line and dealing with this as early as possible will improve a lot of people's lives. The only constant is change and while a lot of our emotional concerns are about what happens around us, we need to try to get into the frame of mind that doesn't fear new things: there is great benefit in seeing them as opportunities, rather than threats. We have become uncomfortable with silence – a time when the body and mind can recharge and reflect. We are continually bombarded by emails, texts, calls and adverts of every conceivable type which has led many of us to get divorced from our real feelings and wants.

Can Stress Be Good?

I was never one of those kids that tried to pack in lots of revision for exams at the last minute. This was for a couple of reasons: firstly, I didn't feel as bright as the others so needed to start earlier. Secondly, I always felt more anxious not doing anything when an exam was imminent. This would encourage me to sit down, open the books and try to make sense of things. Most of my friends preferred to burn the midnight oil close to the big day and felt they worked better this way. It was as if they could think more clearly under a bit of pressure. Without the impact of a looming deadline, they would not go that extra mile or really get down to the task at hand. That opens up the notion that some of us actually need an amount of tension or pressure in order to do things or push back the barriers.

The people I admire most have a built-in stubborn streak, not always apparent but it's there, bubbling under the surface. The desire to succeed where others have faltered is buried deep within them. This is usually considered a good thing but in the context of our over-worked lives, it isn't always as positive as we would like. A bull-headed inability to distinguish between different kinds of demand, burden and pulls on our time, can easily take things out of perspective. Corporate culture seems to have rewarded and elevated those that seem able to work best under pressure, instead of understanding that most of the negative feelings are actually caused by that person and not the remit of the role they are performing.

Perhaps we should be rewarding those that do not put themselves into consistently stressful situations or who look for ways to reduce trauma and add calmness to the workplace. I'm sure we have all seen how one person under stress can affect others, in exactly the same way as a person who spends twelve hours a day at his desk can adversely influence others. If we can help develop a culture where diffusing tension and promoting composure is rewarded, we will get happier people, greater productivity and a better chance of success.

'Stress has risen across the board in all occupations, and is now cited by 36% of professional, 34% of managers and 22% of skilled workers.' Madeleine Bunting, *Willing Slaves*

Big Sleep

We all tend to take our health for granted. I was chatting to a publishing colleague who believes health is the most important thing we can directly affect when we reach 50 years of age. This gem should be prefaced by his tip for reducing stress: drink more, and his tip for improving happiness: drink less. Every time the television is turned on we are told not to eat this and should drink more of that. Rarely are we told that the lack of adequate sleep, especially when we are busy at work or if a deadline is causing concern, can lead to serious emotional and productivity problems. A good sleep will park those bits of information and random emotions that are spinning round our brains at a million miles an hour. Sleep helps us to put them in the correct filing cabinet so we are able to process things in the right order and thereby improve our overall judgment.

Some rules are made to be broken and we can take alcohol as an example. Women are supposed to drink a maximum of 14 units a week and guys 21 units. This is based on a unit being half a pint of beer or a medium-sized glass of wine. I am not averse to a drop of alcohol on occasions and it has been interesting to visit parts of the world where drink is seen differently. I remember turning up to the chic Santa Monica head offices of MGM, feeling a little worse for wear. I had been celebrating with some good friends and could well have had one too many. The attitude to my slightly liverish behaviour and second trip to the 'restroom' in half an hour was extraordinary. It was as if I had committed a terrible crime against humanity and was half expecting to be thrown off the premises without delay. The senior execs I was meeting really didn't get the whole thing about having a blast and letting your hair down once in a while. This particular episode also taught me that good things can come from bad. The impact of the hangover was bad, very bad but I was remembered by all those execs and we still laugh about it today.

Intolerance

It is a fact that the older we get, the more prone we are to developing intolerances and allergies that can effect our performance in the office. One friend of mine in his mid-forties developed an intolerance to dust and by simply replacing the carpets with wood flooring managed to cut out the symptoms almost totally. He worked at home most of the time and saw his productivity and energy levels rise significantly. I went to see a nutritionist, filled out some forms and had some tests. I wasn't sure what my expectations were, perhaps cut down on those upmarket crisps, which I find virtually impossible to resist or maybe eat more greens. The results came back and I seemed to have a reasonably robust constitution in terms of processing fatty foods and alcohol (phew!) but my circulation was being increasingly clogged by wheat and yeast. This stuff had become a big part of my diet, made much worst by my working patterns (such as sandwiches at the desk, coffee and croissants before a meeting, etc.) so it was beginning to cause real problems. I was advised to cut my wheat and yeast intake by 75%, including having pasta only once a week, no bread with meals and as few pre-made sandwiches as possible. The effects were really impressive and I now have more energy and can focus for longer periods.

Fear of Losing Your Job

A large proportion of workers try to avoid redundancy by working extra hours. It's one of the great ironies in our careers, that the longer we spend at our desks, the more exhausted and less productive we usually become. This downward spiral is often accompanied by sleeping or eating disorders, higher levels of aggression and fragmentation of work relationships. Trust and communication can break down as many become gatekeepers of information, rather than passing it on for the benefit of all. Confidence and decision-making become adversely affected, making the whole situation worse. If you feel drawn into this trap, try the following:

* Chat to your boss and other trusted colleagues about your concerns.
* Promote honesty all the time.
* Keep eating well and exercise more.
* Use your support network as things are rarely as bad as they appear.
* Don't work too hard and look out for the signs of over-work.
* Try to foster a spirit of teamworking and togetherness.
* Help someone else.
* Be positive and look for alternatives.

'Don't limit yourself. Many limit themselves to what they think they can do. You can go as far as your mind lets you. What you believe, remember, you can achieve.'
Mary Kay Ash

Sometimes losing your job can open new doors and be the start of an exciting new chapter. One friend of mine had six months gardening leave and wasn't allowed to do any paid work. He had never struck me as the sort who would jump into charity work, but that's exactly what he did and it helped him find a new job. His next employer was incredibly impressed at what he had achieved during that period. The spell as a volunteer really helped to broaden his horizons and he is now a much better team player and manager of people and is happier to boot.

Is Stress Simply the Price of Success?

The higher the salary, the greater probability we will be affected by some level of anxiety, worry or stress disorder. It does seem strange the more we earn and the better status we may hold (i.e. the more successful we are from most people's perspective), the more we are likely to get an adverse mental or emotional reaction. After receiving a couple of promotions in quick succession I had less time to do what I liked and was good at. Both are unsurprising but a sad reflection on workplace success. I had a job with a bigger desk, a good salary and all the trimmings but I no longer enjoyed the day-to-day detail. I also had a whole bunch of new tasks and responsibilities that I wasn't very good at and had to spend a large part of my time sorting out other people's problems rather than being creative, for a start. Signing employee expense forms, their application to go on holiday, performance appraisals, budgets and more budgets, plus a host of other tasks felt like a demotion, not the opposite. I had expected to have more time for strategic thinking, furthering business relationships and getting big deals done. Although there was a bit of that, most of the time I spent doing things which didn't challenge me and certainly didn't make me more fulfilment. If this was success, I wasn't sure I wanted it! It was time to make a big change and see what was on the other side of that work–life seesaw.

Autonomy and Control

Autonomy and Control

The paradox about getting higher up the company tree is the expectation of more autonomy, but often we get less. I like autonomy. I like the feeling of being in some kind of control no matter how small a task might be, rather than always being a small cog in a large wheel. Much of the time I have made decisions in my career that acknowledge this. When we are in charge of a small team or just ourselves, objectives are easily identifiable and therefore achievement levels are often clear-cut. We can see the impact of what we achieve immediately. As soon as the situation became more complicated, where we have influence over lots of people, more business activities and often a less clearly defined area of responsibility, the feeling that we are actually adding to the process can get very lost.

One of the most remarkable changes to our working lives and our ability to think about what we are actually doing, is pace. Just a few short years ago, business wasn't played out at the speed of thought, it was more at the speed of the fax machine or the postman. We had time to evaluate, assess and weigh up the options as individuals and see decisions as part of a greater whole. This seems no longer possible as computer and software technology are 'helping' us to be much more immediately reactive. I never feel completely comfortable with being asked to make a snap judgment, and later in the day usually wish I had added additional comment or perspective. I will make a quick decision and it doesn't worry me when I make a bad one, but having to continually react without due consideration doesn't make me a better businessman at all. I totally understand that the speed of business can be important in getting a competitive advantage but I'm just not sure how much reward it really gives us, or the company, in the long run. This is also a disease that is spreading wildly out of control. We have only got to be on a train at the start or end of a day to see people clicking away at palm-sized devices, laptops or mobile phones, to see that we are being sucked into a frenzied techno-wonderland.

Blame Culture

I'm sure we are all guilty of playing the blame game at times. Something goes disastrously wrong and we point the finger. Every firm that I have worked with that has a blame culture, is also defensive and slightly paranoid about moving away from the *status quo*. Persecuted managers become more con-servative and a feeling grows that staff could get fired for making the wrong decision, so there is a tendency to make no decision or get someone else to make the call. This is the worst of all worlds as it means we don't get the rewards of doing good, new things and are continually worried about something going wrong with what little we have achieved. My view has always been that any decision is better than no decision. To stand still means we are actually falling behind, because others are moving and we get little new information either. This is a lose-lose situation!

I often try to inject some humour when things go wrong. It doesn't always work and I am far from being a funny guy, but it hopefully shows that I haven't taken things too seriously. That alone can go a long way to helping the poor soul who knows he's dropped a clanger. I also try to depersonalise the whole situation, taking it away from a single person or team and into the much bigger realm where ever possible. Getting lots of people thinking and looking for a new solution, not only helps everyone look forward, it also gives the sense we are not alone when things go wrong. There is nothing worse than feeling isolated. It is like being back at school and having to make the long walk to the headmaster's office or sit on the naughty step.

The Wrong Place

Fatigue is another readily identifiable result of taking the wrong approach to our working lives. It can creep up on us slowly but the feeling of no energy or drive can have a negative impact on all concerned. In my early years of working, I thought people with less get-up-and-go, just needed a bigger stick or a fatter carrot. I really didn't understand this might be the result of stress, unhappiness or dissatisfaction. There was an accounts manager who worked for me and always looked down in the mouth. Rarely did I see a smile and always looked like she just got out of bed the wrong side. At a company event, I made a point of chatting to her and tried to find out more. It turned out she went for a promotion, didn't get it and consequently felt over-looked and undervalued. I couldn't give her a better job as there were lots of good people in the department doing well so I came up with a different idea. I would give her more work! I had a few projects outside of the core business that needed some numbers crunching along with some analysis and informed her boss of this, xplaining my reasons. I then got the lady in and said I had chosen her personally to do some important work for me and many of the projects were quite confidential. She shouldn't go around dis-cussing the contents because it might impact on others in the business. I gave her quite a short time in which to complete the first task and all the relevant paperwork. Several good things came out of this exercise beyond getting someone way more experienced in this field to run some numbers; the lady in question felt important again and the odd smile did return. I managed to have a direct relationship with her without putting others people's noses out of joint and her energy levels suddenly came back as well.

'Hard work never killed anyone, but I figure, why take the chance.'
Ronald Reagan

Blood and Sweat

Blood and Sweat

On a trip to Hong Kong, I was out walking in a park quite close to the centre and became transfixed by 20 or so quite elderly Chinese people performing Tai Chi. It was remarkably graceful and rhythmical, if unusual to the untrained Western eye. I was intrigued and decided to find out more. To many people in the Far East, this form of exercise provides a way of keeping limbs and muscles extremely supple, plus fostering a sharpened relationship between mind and body. I tried it and made a complete mess of just about every move but got the feeling this could be a very different way to look at exercising our bodies. Many of those performing talked of the harmony and greater connection felt between body and mind, which seemed very powerful to them. I'm not suggesting we should all go down to our local park and synchronise movements, but we might be rewarded by finding something similar that works for us.

Looking at something new for the body can be just as important as stimulating the mind, if the benefits of change are to be harnessed fully. Many of us put our bodies at risk with too much work and poor diets along with a lack of exercise and only try to do something about it when it's late in the day. I am a great supporter of looking at what many call alternative therapies and treatments such as reflexology, acupuncture, yoga, pilates, aromatherapy, massage and meditation. They may not work for everyone but the process of trying to understand where they come from and what they have to offer is a huge value in itself. I worked on an exercise DVD series with a popular instructor called Katy Appleton and we met one evening to discuss her latest project. She was a fascinating person and had just come back from an extensive trip to Northern India. She had spent ten days in a monastery, practicing an ancient system of meditation, where she wasn't allowed to speak to anyone for a whole week. She would sit in the same, trance-like position for days at a time, to a point where she thought she might go completely mad before finding a place of true mental peace. This, I was told, was quite normal. It sounded like an amazing experience and she is now able to go to that place in her mind virtually anytime she needs to. It is as if she is now able to unlock the door of real calm and peace, a place that once she knew where it was, could visit when necessary. This is a tremendous comfort to her.

Personal Profile – Mike

Background – Mike runs a very successful family business, started by his father in 1944 and is proud of the fact that it still operates pretty much as it did all those years ago, even through these challenging times. This situation has engendered a deep sense of responsibility to those connected with the company – family members, staff, many suppliers and others connected with the day-to-day operation. He enjoys being the captain of the ship and welcomes the responsibility, feeling also that it is vital to be able to delegate to keep operating well. This guy is really good with people. He strikes up meaningful relationships and always comes across with the utmost of integrity; one person put this into words for me, 'he doesn't challenge people, just engages with them'.

Success – part of the success equation in his business life is steering the ship on a steady course, rather than rapid growth or diversification into new, potentially more risky, areas. He very much likes to be busy and is never totally happy when business is quiet. The quality of his relationships is a central feature of how success is measured as this is one of the major reasons people do business with him over other companies, even if they are more competitive on price. Many of these relationships have built up over twenty or more years and are based on trust and mutual respect. Financial security is a big motivator and he dislikes debt other than when absolutely necessary. He doesn't worry about what others think or the need to compare himself with peers, putting this down to a sizeable dose of bloody-mindedness. Often time spent comparing our lot and supposed level of success against others has a far from positive impact on our state of mind and outlook.

Work Balance – Mike feels that his leisure time is very valuable because he spends quite a lot of time in the same office. He avoids taking work home, so he can properly unwind and relax. Mike is no early adopter when it comes to technology and still sees little value in spending lots of time building a website when relationships traditionally have made the difference. Certain operating tasks including accounting and administration have benefited massively from computerised applications but he wants to maintain the speed of response to customers by not getting distracted by other things.

Retirement – succession doesn't seem to be on the cards so an exit is likely to be via a sale of the company. He hasn't given the notion of retirement too much thought as he feels it will take care of itself as long as good decisions are made beforehand.

Advice – always try to empathise with people and there point of view. Think things through well but then be confident in your decisions and abilities and others will follow suit. Always try to keep your temper and emotions as a good way of managing the highs and lows that we go through. Having consistent norms and values over time is a huge benefit when dealing with others in the business world and his philosophy is to try to earn £10 before spending £1.

Addicted to Adrenalin

One growing trend I have watched closely with some alarm is the number of hard-working executives who are becoming addicted to the 'rush'. The sheer velocity with which their lives are moving becomes like a drug they can't live without. Normal things we all should enjoy become less important and this ends up affecting relationships, friends and just about everything. It is like any other drug, it grabs hold of the mind and proves difficult to shift. If you are in this category or are teetering on the edge, act fast. Look at ways to re-balance your lifestyle and outlook, throw out as much of the old as you can and look back at what used to make you happy. I'm sure the same calm person is still inside, but perhaps has been on holiday for a while, distracted by things that aren't important after all. Running headlong into business situations, usually results in poorer performance at work ain the long run nd far less harmony with the social life.

Pride of Performance

Are you proud of what you do? If you asked others in the office would they be proud of what they achieve both individually and collectively? Many companies are unified by that sense of positive feeling, emanating from the confidence found in pride of performance. Sometimes, a small task can improve the atmosphere and bring people together, galvanising everyone into action. One company I work with always struck me as a very disparate group of individuals, working in different directions, that is until the receptionist organised a fund-raising fun run. To my surprise, virtually everyone took part and it somehow got people working closer together. On a separate occasion, I remember feeling hugely proud of my marketing team's response when we devised a quite unusual promotional campaign for a new interactive product. It was about seeding small video sequences in lots of different places to see if people would be interested to find out more. The following week, I was told by my American boss that we should go down a more conventional route. Their promotional campaign had worked in USA, so they thought that should work in the UK. There wasn't anything I could do but accept the decision and try to get everyone motivated again. This was a campaign that would have to wait a while before being let out!

A Better You

Bestselling author Joel Osteen wrote a book entitled *Become a Better You – 7 Keys to Improving Your Life Every Day* and it was a pretty big hit across the pond. I liked his introduction, 'Whether life is going well for you or collapsing right before your eyes, we all want to be better. We want to be more effective in our lives'. It's quite a powerful point, and something with which I totally empathise. In his book, the seven keys are as follows:
* Keep pressing forward.
* Be positive towards yourself.
* Develop better relationships.
* Form better habits.
* Embrace the place where you are.
* Develop your inner life.
* Stay passionate about life.

Much of the basis of this book is believing that we actually create much of our own unhappiness ourselves. If we are able to stop fighting against the things we can't change or worrying about the things that have already happened, we can usually improve the situation dramatically.

We should also try to accept the place where we are right now and that doesn't just mean our physical surroundings. Staying passionate about life is much easier said than done, especially when the tide seems to be flowing against us. It's important in these times to focus on positive aspects and really appreciate the good stuff such as having a delicious meal with friends or seeing something new for the first time.

'Always walk through life as if you have something new to learn and you will.' Vernon Howard

Work Boundaries

In *The Secrets of CEOs*, the authors interview a whole bunch of corporate leaders. Although these captains of industry have experienced a great deal of success in the boardroom, rarely have they had what anyone would call a balanced existence. They quote 'The happiest CEOs we've met are those who have managed either to build strong boundaries between their work and home lives, so that home refreshes them for work and work does not impinge on home; or those who have fully integrated their work and their personal lives and do not see a massive tension between the two'. I have also picked out some suggestions as to what CEOs should do to avoid getting bogged down in the corporate mire:

1) Make time for you as well as the business.
2) Know what can refresh you daily.
3) Set simple rules that impose structure on your life.
4) Be as serious about time 'off' as time 'on'.
5) Build an active support network.
6) Family and friends keep you grounded.

Labels

I found a review of a fascinating social experiment in *Self Matters* by Phillip C. McGraw, which reads as follows: 'Many years ago, a team of psychologists launched a research project using grade school students as subjects. The researchers were looking at how the social environment, and specifically the treatment one receives from those perceived as powerful and relevant, affects a person's self-concept. At the beginning of the school year, the researchers separated a class of sixth graders into two groups. The selection process was carefully randomised so that the two groups of kids would be virtually identical in terms of average intelligence, ability, maturity level, background, and so on.

The researchers then told one group that they were the Bluebirds, exceptional children who had been identified as having unusually high ability. They were told that the work that year would be challenging and the pace would be rapid, in keeping with their special gifts. Across the hall, by contrast, the Yellow Birds were told that they were going to face many challenges; and that the school year was likely to be a struggle for many of them, but that their teacher was going to try their hardest to help each one of them. The message to the Yellow Birds was basically, 'You're marginally bright, and your achievements in life are going to be marginal, at best.' Every other aspect of their experience was identical. All of the students, regardless of their group categorisation, received exactly the same assignments, followed the same schedule, and took the same tests.

Thankfully, this kind of project would probably die today while still in the proposal stage. These days, you cannot and should not get approval for a psychological study that poses a risk of harm to the participants. Sure enough, although artificial division of this class lasted only four months, the consequences were profound and went on for years. The Yellow Birds did, in fact struggle and showed serious frustration and self-recrimination associated with their difficulties. Unfortunately, the troubles did not end when the label was removed. When the researchers again looked at these children ten years later, the kids who had been Yellow Birds had consistently earned significantly poorer grades, were much less successful in activities like sports and music, were more likely to have trouble with the law, and scored significantly lower on intelligence tests that the Bluebirds.'

The label that we get given, often in a random way, can have a tremendously powerful influence on our lives. The labels given by us to others can be equally significant and will shape attitudes and behaviour. Sometimes we give ourselves labels, which, if we can't shrug them off, can hold us back in every part of our life.

'To employ yourself can be a step towards freedom.' Jeanne Marine, Actress

Personal Profile – Shaun

Background – he is an associate of one of the world's largest search and recruitment firms and spends a great deal of time evaluating others' career aims, objectives, motivations and talents. This often seems easier than looking at his own career. He studied law, getting quite close to becoming qualified before having second thoughts. He wasn't getting the sense of achievement expected, so took the decision to switch careers in his twenties.

Success – Shaun enjoys people interaction. He feeds off meeting different characters and thoroughly enjoys being a headhunter. He feels that many professions, especially doctors, solicitors and accountants have an extremely linear learning path, making it more difficult to step into something new if one gets too far down the road. All reference points are in one very specific area. For many that he comes into contact with in business, the path of least resistance has a significant impact on what that person does for a living, which doesn't often lead to harmony. Success for him is about enjoying what he does each week; being able to shape his own destiny to some degree and not have to make decisions based solely on monetary factors. Personal integrity is very important, being able to look people in the eye knowing you have worked hard, done your best and acted in a very open manner. Technology has helped a great deal in communicating with people on the go, especially when he is travelling on business. Keeping several search projects moving forward at the same time is vital as many can take months to complete. There are now several established Internet-based recruitment companies that are directly competing with the traditional search model. He feels, however, this will only affect certain levels of job and people interaction will prevail for the vast majority of clients searching for good new staff.

Work Balance – he is now based in Switzerland, where they have a very different attitude to work–life balance. There are few dinner engagements or late meetings and colleagues rarely encroach on personal time. People still care about what they do, but feel that having a proper balance is good for everyone in the long run. He has learnt that the ability to manage his time effectively in all aspects of his life has enabled him to squeeze all the things he needs into each week.

Retirement – if Shaun had to put a number on the retirement age he would like it would be 55, although he would need to feel financially comfortable at that stage to pack in the day job. He has always liked to challenge himself and sees retirement as just another phase to test himelf. The actual elements will be different and will depend on family and friends, but the same desire will prevail.

Advice – don't get stressed about events that are outside of our control and if things go wrong, it's just a matter of working out how to sort them out.

Act Like an Entrepreneur

I was at a party a while ago and began chatting to a French banker who specialised in working with Chinese companies in their development into Europe. After a few minutes, he was talking about how different cultures embrace change differently and he was certainly in a good position to judge. It started me thinking about the mental process I go through in looking at new things, so I asked a series of successful businessmen and women what they thought. The consensus can be broadly summarised as follows:

Step 1 – start with a concept or even sometimes just the germ of an idea.

Step 2 – develop the concept and look at it from all angles. Visualise the idea as a logo, brand, website or service and obtain some reaction from people you trust.

Step 3 – cost the idea and try to forecast what will need to be spent each month until the cash coming in will exceed cash flowing out.

Step 4 – do a deal, as a business idea is only testable when dropped into the commercial world. Foster a 'can do' approach to just about everything.

Step 5 – look to move the initial perspective forward, often with partners, suppliers or to a larger customer base. Make the commercial platform solid.

Step 6 – build a team and see how much equity you need to forgo to reach your objective.

Step 7 – look to whether you want to run a bigger business or step back. Do you need to be hands-on?

Step 8 – make sure you have a life.

Are You Ready for a Change?

Here are some pointers about when and how to implement a shift in thinking:

* Vacation blues – try not to make a major decision within a month of returning from a holiday. The world always looks different and rarely better after a dose of sunshine, exploring, skiing, etc. A new life needs to be sustainable by you.

* Career aims – list your long-term work goals and whether you can achieve all or most of them within your current business. This will give you a good idea about whether you should be staying put.

* Moving around – have you moved more than three times in the last ten years or so and is this above average for your industry? If you have, analyse the reasons for moving to see if they are still valid or even more pertinent.

* Change list – make a list of the things you would like to change in your life and prioritise them. If there are not many items that are directly related to work, then changing your career path is probably not going to solve anything. You may need to look elsewhere for solutions.

* Advice – recruitment consultants, friends in human resources, companies advertising jobs – chat to them all and ask for candid feedback.

Positive Mental Outlook

Positive Mental Outlook

In many parts of the world, Great Britain in particular, optimism and being confrontational with business issues are often viewed with amazing amounts of suspicion. Most entrepreneurs I have met have one thing in common: the ability to see how things could happen if some focused effort was applied. In other words, an optimistic outlook. If we all got caught up in the mire of pessimism, we would still be living in caves. In Laurence Shorter's book, *The Optimist – one man's search for the brighter side of life*, he outlines four ways to an optimism manifesto:

'1) New optimists see all events as positive.

2) It is not events such as losing our job, nuclear war, repossession that we are afraid of, nor our reactions to them; we're afraid of our feelings.

3) If we don't resist them, feelings have their own life cycle – they come and go without doing harm.

4) Happiness is a decision – we can have it now, or we can wait for it to 'happen' to us some time in the future when the conditions are right.'

Body Clock

Body Clock

Our body clock is a fantastic piece of biological machinery. Ignoring it effectively means we are pushing against ourselves and many of our natural instincts. Every one of us has our own individual body clock, but most follow similar patterns, and understanding them can help us achieve more in our work and the rest of our lives. As an example, two glasses of wine have far more impact at lunchtime than in the evening because our body temperature is higher in the late afternoons. Many Olympic and high-endurance athletes undertake their really intensive workouts in the afternoon because the body can cope more easily due to its temperature change. Many people exercise in the morning, which is a time when we are at our most mentally strong and manually dexterous. The best time to exercise is actually 4pm–7pm when our mind and body start to struggle with what they have to consume. In terms of eating, the trend towards consuming larger meals later in the day is a much more modern day phenomenon than most think, giving the body lots to digest when it is slowing down. This has certainly affected obesity levels. Our mental and physical performance would be much better if the balance was to have more calories for breakfast than at supper. Identifying aspects of our own body clock can be a big advance in business and achieving more from our lives in general.

Final Thoughts – The Mental Battle

At the start of each year I try to put a list together of new things to explore or learn more about. I like the concept of not just drifting through another twelve months without finding out more about something potentially valuable to keep me sharp. Occasionally the topics are niche and other times they require in-depth research and study. Some things fit into the category of social interests or hobbies but I also like to have workplace-related areas as well. If you are able to find out a lot more about just one new thing, it could help open the door to lots of other things as well. Some of the key thoughts from this chapter are as follows:

– Work separation – find out whether you are happier separating work and your social life or integrating everything fully. There is rarely much room in the middle.

– High stress – our working lives encourage greater levels of stress and anxiety than ever before, eroding our confidence and levels of self-esteem. See the signs and head things off early.

– Adrenalin – if you are becoming addicted to the rush of the workplace, it's time to go 'cold-turkey'.

– Take charge – keep moving forward, form better habits and build more constructive relationships. We can't control many things in the outside business world but we can influence how we respond.

– Label – descriptions can affect our state of mind and we therefore have to be aware when and how to put a marker on someone or something.

Random Mind Matter

* Sarkozy's energy – how do leading politicians and business people round the world find the energy levels to work seventy-plus hours a week, go through long spells of sleep deprivation and seemingly go from one crisis to another. I always thought it must be down to

some kind of drug. The day you step into the big office the civil servant comes round with a string of small objects that look like Smarties. I'm sure reality is slightly different and in the case of Nicolas Sarkozy, there is evidence to prove that there is something that helps him maintain those phenomenal energy level. Regular manual therapy (no, not what you are thinking!) dispensed from an alternative medicine specialist called Jean-Paul Moureau. The treatment involves lots of back massage and transference of positive energy waves. While you might sense the slight air of scepticism in my tone, I do think that looking at getting new and different treatments should be on everyone's agenda. Our bodies are complicated things and the more attention we lavish on them, the better they will run. This isn't just about looking at our bodies in isolation but finding a place where body and mind fuse together to produce synergy and greater output.

* Do You Feel Trapped By Your Job? – how does this feeling manifest itself? Can you isolate these feelings and their impact in order to recognise the exact effects and be better prepared when things are not good?

* Life chain – think of your life as a chain, a series of connected stages where what you are today has been affected by what has gone on in all previous phases. It means that as humans we have a mental continuity and although the past may be a good indicator of how you are likely to approach things, it's possible to significantly influence future steps. Understanding how we approach things and what influences us is key to our evolution as human beings.

* Extend your life – a Scottish Mental Health survey found that we could on average add four years to our lives if we had good, regular sex. If you want to increase the chances of living to 100, then you should move to Okinawa in Japan or Sardinia, as they have the highest ratio of centenarians on the planet. If that seems a little extreme, try to increase the amount of oily fish, fibre and fruit you eat instead.

* Trading places – bartering everyday produce, skills and foodstuffs used to be a big part of society and not just in the history books before money really got going, but more recently too. We would trade with others, we would offer people something and they would offer us goods or services in return. There may have been some haggling about that exchange but a deal was done which

benefited both sides. The next time you have to make a corporate purchase, enlist an outside company or dip into the cash reserves, have a think about whether there might be someone out there willing to trade or barter with you. Perhaps you have a service that they might want, an area of technical expertise, which has some value outside your walls or an item that has more value to someone else. This also applies to personal situations; if you can't sell your house, possessions, second-hand car or antique furniture, try to swap it for something you do need. Given the ease with which many people can communicate these days (Facebook, Twitter, eBay, LinkedIn, etc. let alone simple-old email) putting deals together is no longer time-consuming or problematic.

7 A Wealth of Ideas

Aim

Money is the fuel necessary to run many of the elements of our lives. We can make the best of our financial position by looking at the financial habits of successful people, identifying common cash-related problems to avoid and working out what issues need to be tackled head-on. We can't all be accountants, fantastic mathematicians or think like bank managers (sadly!) but we can all make better financial decisions and look at ways to reverse that feeling of money running through our fingers.

'There are risks and costs to a programme of action. But they are far less than the long-range risks and costs of comfortable inaction.'
J.F. Kennedy

More Options

We need to understand that making different financial decisions will give us more options in many aspects of our career and life. There are rarely short-term fixes but there are plenty of ways to improve our financial health over time. Money can't buy you love (or so the song goes) but is another important area where we can aim to improve. We have become more than a little used to the creature comforts funded by a certain amount of cash and often don't know the real costs of some of these 'essentials'. This isn't a book about how to retire with a million in the bank, but there are some useful tips about cash management from some pretty successful people. After all, it doesn't seem sensible to work hard and receive a good salary, if it doesn't lead to more happiness, contentment and tangible reward.

Money and Happiness

There are times in our lives when achieving better balance is about access to money. The knowledge that bills can get paid, you can build a nest-egg for the future or can help someone else, which means we can be more positive about other aspects of our life. It's certainly never easy to be creative or innovative when worried about the date the salary gets paid in each month or how many pages the credit card bill will run to. I am a firm believer that getting the finances sorted out provides for many people, better conditions for work–life balance. Although financial necessity can be the mother of invention, it can also be the root cause of much pain, anxiety and suffering. I know which side I sit on in this debate.

Baggage

The whole concept of cash comes with a lot of baggage. Our attitude towards money is formed predominantly in our early years and is based on learned behaviour from our family. I'm sure if our parents knew how those discussions over pocket-money might shape our life, they might have taken a bit more time to think things through. Many people put the bank manager in a special category with the likes of traffic wardens and dentists, as people to be avoided at all costs. How can this be? They don't inflict physical pain or suffering, and most money problems are caused by ourselves, not them. Perhaps the issue is more to do with our fear of money issues than the bastion who looks after it. Or maybe it's that the humble bank manager stands for everything logical, an authority figure who points the finger if we misbehave or can't understand things that we really should. Either way, getting the most from your bank and their personnel is one of the things people with money do better. I have never found banks easy to deal with or understand and they can be remarkable unhelpful. They are huge organisations that seem to employ staff who are woefully under trained in how to deal with people and problem situations. This is slightly strange as it's the basis of a bank's existence.

Like a Hobby

Looking after money is like any favourite hobby; the more we practice it, the better we will become. Rarely will being lethargic bring the best results and it can prove expensive. Banks can be a source of help but this relationship like all others, needs to be managed closely. As a good example, most banks have a whole range of financial products on offer, the vast majority of which we never really know about, unless we push them for information. We need to continually ask questions of our money managers in order to be aware of what services are available: I start from the perspective that individuals often don't know what they have until I make them check their cupboard, that way I'm less likely to be disappointed.

Personal Profile – Cal

Background – has been highly successful, working his way up in the world of big business within just two companies (rare these days) for almost 25 years. There is a strong bread-winner mentality and sense of family, as he talks about the sacrifice of his parents for him to have a better start in life. He enjoys work: the pace and the cut-and-thrust but feels he operates better within his comfort zone. He has identified being happiest when making decisions within his area of expertise.

Success – Cal believes the reason we work, at its most basic level, is to fund other parts of our life. The starting point is to have a secure, fully-funded home which is the thing that no-one can then take away, no matter what goes wrong. The need for financial security, along with fear of failure continue to play a major role in his career route. Ultimately success can be measured in two ways, the hard or physical assets such as having a nice house, and then the soft elements. These are much more about respect from peers, family and friends plus our own view of where we fit into society and whether we are actually adding something to our environment. For example, a charity worker is unlikely to be able to afford a big house but will get a lot of respect from those around them. He feels we all need to get the right mix of these two measures to be fulfilled.

Work Balance – working for a corporation means lots of day-to-day things are outside our control and influence, often giving a sense of real powerlessness, even when high up in the food chain. Achieving vice-president level at forty has provided a great many experiences that wouldn't have otherwise been possible but they have come at a cost. Social life certainly came second at many times of his life. He could not consider a sabbatical or change of direction until financially secure, but if he was made redundant, would probably embrace the change.

Retirement – Cal defines this period as one when we don't need to worry about having to generate money. For him, it couldn't start until the mortgage had been paid off and had fully understood what kind of lifestyle he wanted. Cal feels there are definitely three stages in life for most of us: education, then the working phase and finally, moving into retirement. He would like to retire as early as possible, but it must be on the right footing. Retirement is about spending quality time, doing things that we really want to do and having time to relax and think. Not trying to cram things into a hectic schedule is definitely a goal, along with having the time to really appreciate what's going on around him. Retirement is possibly a time when all those ideas and notions that have been kept locked up in a closed box, come out and are developed. Technology enslaves most people, exposing us to the culture of complete availability. For him, there has been a growing level of intrusion coupled with a lack of control. As an example, the open diary system on his company's intranet means that anyone with authority can put things into his schedule, leaving him less time to be proactive. We are also suffering from information overload, receiving far more than we can possibly consume, so somehow we need to develop a natural sifting process. He has seen a growing and alarming trend towards an inability to express things in written form, and this is also part of a larger problem of an erosion of social and communication skills. Technology has played a large part in making us less involved with others and living our lives at arms length from those close to us. **Advice** – we somehow need to ask ourselves regularly what we are good at and what we are looking for from our working life. If we can be confident that we are good at much of what we are doing, we will do it better and expand our horizons.

Money Matters

It's always good to know where the hell we are heading and our finances are no different. To get more peace of mind, we need to have an idea of where we want to be in the short-, medium- and longer term. This doesn't mean getting down to the nitty-gritty of a cashflow forecast every week, just need to examine where we feel comfortable. For example, if you are concerned about having enough money to pay the bills in forthcoming months, then open a new account and set up a standing order each month. It's a very small action but our financial health is usually about making lots of positive steps rather than one big leap.

Many of us use expensive short-term borrowing, either on credit or store cards or a quick overdraft or loan to fund a lifestyle. Rarely do those who understand wealth creation fall into this trap. It's tough to get out of and even if we are able to do so, the resulting impact on the pocket is always high. A goal could well be to turn these short-term facilities into longer-term debt. The key is to make a plan where income exceeds outgoings and stick to it for a period of months, a year or perhaps longer. It's also worth building a little slack in your plan in case of an emergency. I haven't met anyone yet who doesn't like the feeling of security in having some-thing put aside for that rainy day; we just need to realise that this 'luxury' is usually at the expense of some aspects of our current lifestyle.

I never had a burning desire to be super-rich or have a million pounds in the bank, I just didn't want to have to worry about how to pay any bill that came under the door. My first meeting with a bank manager was on my sixteenth birthday and, armed with cash that was given as a present, I ploughed into the nearest bank and asked to open an account. In those days, we usually got to see the manager and I dutifully went into a room that had a striking resemblance to a headmaster's office. The grey-suited, formal chap said that he couldn't offer me an overdraft, so I immediately replied, that I didn't want his money as I had my own. It was a simple statement and I didn't think much about it at the time but I instinctively didn't like the feeling of being beholden to this miserable-looking guy or anyone like him. If he had my money, he had to be nice to me, not the other way round.

Too Lazy

Richard Templar in his book, *The Rules of Wealth*, states, 'most people are too lazy to be wealthy'. This may be true for some but it does not help any of us very much. There is absolutely no point running like mad in the wrong direction where money is concerned. Knowing where to go and the best decisions to make is vital. Money isn't one of those commodities that get handed out to the best people or those that deserve it. It doesn't often get given to the people who work the hardest either. And, if we do see cash as the universal panacea for all problems, we are likely to become very disillusioned very quickly. Somehow we need to acquire more of it without lifting our expectations of what it will do for us.

'God helps those who help themselves.' Benjamin Franklin

Dispelling the Money Myths

We all have preconceived notions of wealth and these often have their foundations in the notion that making money somehow turns us into bad people. To some minds, staying poor means we are much better, more ethical, caring, environmentally friendly and honest! I have seen many people with varying degrees of this illness. Trying to increase the bank balance doesn't turn us into ruthless or greedy people overnight, we are not selling our soul to the devil or compromising our morals. We can all be better with money, be happier, enjoy our careers and get a good night's sleep at the same time. It's just about deciding what you want and how much is enough. More wealth gives us options and if we use it to help others, go greener or just be less stressed, then that doesn't mean we are some kind of Ebenezer Scrooge.

People with Money

During much of my early life, I really looked up to people who had money; in my eyes they must have done great deeds, created wonderful inventions or been hugely clever. As I came to know more people with wealth, I realised they were similar to the rest of us. Similar but not identical! They had habits that often looked fairly small and irrelevant on their own but which gave them insight into the world of the well-to-do. They knew how the game was played and many were students of the art of money management. This was something I decided I had to learn as I didn't want to be left behind. I tasked myself with finding out the language and jargon of interest rates, exchange rates, pensions, savings plans and tax saving measures, ways of making money work while we slept and so on. It is not a place full of belly laughs, but can provide some great satisfaction and mental reward.

Depreciating Assets

One of the differences between successful types and the rest of us is what I call a desire for depreciating assets. If we split our possessions into two categories, there are those that are likely to go up in value such as houses, paintings and investments, and those which usually fall in value. These include cars, computers, home furnishings, etc. I asked a number of people what the true cost of their car was and got an amazing diversity of answers. Obviously most of us need a car but do we know the real cost of it. If we did, we might think again about this decision. One colleague bought a new car three years ago for around £20,000 and borrowed 50%. He now wants to sell the car and is likely to get around £7,000 for it. With the cost of the debt included, this car has cost him over £5,000 per year – nearly £100 per week, excluding running costs such as road tax, petrol, servicing, insurance, etc. If he had bought a similar model second-hand for £10,000, he would have saved himself a sizable £8,000 over the same period. Apply this over a 20-year period and the result is a saving of well over £50,000.

If we were asked what our really biggest cost items were over the last ten years, we might think about our house, car, dining room table, etc. But the true answer might be different as we can all get confused by the original cost of something compared to its actual monetary value. I have been pretty lucky with property and made money on virtually every home I have bought. Given that I have not lost money, these purchases can't really be considered a cost item at all. They are a calculated risk but haven't worked out to be a cost even when borrowing was taken into account. If you have a reliable income, your largest cost in any year could well be your tax bill. If this is so, then it would seem to follow that understanding the intricacies of the glorious tax system, would be a priority. The vast majority of us, however, view the taxman as someone to be avoided at all costs!

I was having lunch with a colleague who was bemoaning the fact that lending rates were coming down very fast, and the adverse impact this was having on his interest income. He was looking at half a dozen different ways of using cash to get better yields over a two- to three-year time horizon. He didn't want to take huge risks but he wasn't satisfied with the sort of returns likely for a while to come. I asked him whether all this effort was ever going to pay off. He had quite a lot of cash at his disposal and I felt all these new ideas were likely to only help his wealth by a very small amount. His reply gave me an insight, as he wanted to maximise the return even when rates were low. This attitude is part of his thought process and actually an important element of his mental make-up that contributes to his self-esteem. I expressed reservations about his possible actions and he said that if I didn't want to be wealthier badly enough, I should become happy at being less well off. Getting wealthy is as much a state of mind, as it is about knowing what proportion of money to put into a tax-efficient saving scheme or pension plan.

'If there is no wind, row'.
thinkexist.com

Getting Started

If you are not great with figures (and any glance at the number of youngsters acquiring mathematic qualifications each year tells us we are not alone) get some help. There are lots of websites and helplines but my experience is these are not very easy to use. The simplest way is to enlist the help of a friend or advisor, someone you trust and to whom you can speak candidly about your money. There are many good independent financial advisors (IFAs) out there but make sure you check out their credentials if you are in any doubt. References are essential. Finding out where you are, what things you have and what immediate options are available, requires just a little technical application. If you are like me, the idea of revealing financial secrets to an outsider doesn't provide a warm feeling, however, obtaining a professional person's input is a hurdle to overcome quickly.

What needs to come out of your evaluation process is a plan of attack. This is not a 20-point dossier of everything you should spend your hard-earned cash on over the next five years, but should focus on a few important steps. Try not to plan too far ahead as the amount of success you have will open or close other doors. As an example, ask yourself whether you would be happier saving and adding to the pension pot or investing in assets such as a bigger house. I was chatting to a businesswoman who was putting quite a large sum into a pension scheme but also running an overdraft and a large mortgage. Now that just seems crazy to me, or at best, hugely optimistic about the value of the pension. This stage is really about taking control of your finances in ways that are right for you. IFAs, on the whole, may be much better at telling you what products are the most tax-efficient but are likely to be less expert at understanding what sort of saver or investor you are. After all, if they were good communicators they would probably be doing something more creative!

You may well have enough money to pay immediate bills, have holidays in nice places and go out to eat when you like, but are you building wealth that will make the future easier? Often this is about stringing together a bunch of good decisions and ensuring you are receiving everything to which you are entitled. This includes maximising income from interest, reducing bank loans or other debt charges, using all tax allowances and subsidies along with focusing your spending on the right things. I have met a lot of people, many of them in the younger generation, who feel they don't have to do a great deal to be rewarded with fame and fortune. Celebrity culture has gripped our society and I truly hope the virus is cured before long lasting damage is done. Unfortunately this is usually a hard lesson to learn for those afflicted!

'Man is made for happiness, not for wealth, and the two are entirely independent of one another and even inimical.' Eric Gill

Perception of Wealth

When you see a really smartly dressed man or woman, do you think that person is successful or not? I'm certainly in the former camp. Either way, people's perceptions of you are likely to be formed before you even utter a word. Based on clothing, the way you carry yourself and your demeanour, others will start to create long-lasting attitudes relating to your abilities, skills and business personality. Why start in the second division when you want to play in the premier league? It just doesn't make sense! We allocate funds to many things in our lives but investing in ourselves shows self-awareness, self-confidence and often some imagination. If we are not prepared to invest in ourself, will others have similar reservations? An outgoing persona should never be a false one and trying to be someone you're not is a big mistake, as the truth will come out. Showing yourself in the best possible light, however, has got to make sense. If Armani or Hugo Boss outfits aren't you, just pick things that have something idiosyncratic or individual about them. Who wants to look like the others? After all, if we want to sell a car, the way to get the best price is to make it gleam and sparkle.

'The future belongs to those who prepare for it today.' Malcolm X

Roulette or Blackjack?
Sceptics consider that investing time in a new project or starting your own company is like gambling. We put money on black and hope it comes up lots of times so the champagne can flow. When starting a business, we put in some money, time, etc. and wait to see if it makes big profit or loss. Most entrepreneurs who have been consistently good at a whole variety of commercial dealings don't look at it that way. Building wealth is never about red or black, it is about changing the odds by making good decisions one after another.

'For every pleasure money is useless.' William Blake

Luck and Risk
You don't have to risk your home, cash reserves or the family silver to be successful. Many of us think ourselves too cautious to ever become successful or wealthy. Being a big gambler is certainly not a guaranteed way to make millions but, at times, taking considered risks is necessary. It's about understanding the level of risk that you enjoy and can cope with, then doing your homework. If that risk level is zero, then fine, it means you have to use different skills to be successful and not compare yourself with others on whom lady-luck has shone. However, I do believe we can't expect to get lucky if we don't take any risks. Life is a risk, getting out of bed is a risk, crossing the road is a risk! Many I have met have the ability to break a complex decision into small elements and find ways to reduce areas they are concerned about or that carry the largest risk.

Personal Profile – Nigel

Background – this guy has had an extraordinary and varied working life, from porter to steeplejack and foreign exchange banker to group chief executive of a multi-national luxury goods business. He now runs his own publishing company and has investments in many richly diverse areas. This gentleman is well into his seventies but his sparkle and appetite for business and life has never diminished.

Success – even though he has amassed considerable wealth, his belief is that success isn't about money. Looking back on his career, what has given most pleasure has been providing young people the opportunity to achieve as well as being able to do things in his own manner. Performing tasks in unconventional ways, often produces results different from others, which he has always put great value on.

Work Balance – he believes there is inherently more stress in today's workplace than in years gone by, fuelled by more responsibility and jealousy of others around us. Hard work should never be stressful if we are doing something enjoyable but he now sees many people who seem allergic to a bit of sweat and toil. Luck for him has been meeting and working with the right people.

Retirement – Nigel can't envisage a time when he stops learning from people or enjoying the buzz of workplace interaction. He enjoys many and varied business activities and if retired, feels he would have less to look forward to.

Advice – I asked what made him move into such different businesses and he believes this is down to his innate curiosity. That being curious about how things work is an absolutely vital ingredient for success in business and life. Cheap things are expensive, as we need to keep replacing them – we should buy the best things we can afford as they will look good and last longer. Even though many of us live in a land of plenty, we should not take things for granted as we will lose track of our mission. He likes optimism and realism in equal measure. Finally, we should read all the time, everything and anything and especially people!

Retirement Plan

Retirement Plan
We are living longer and many of us are hoping to retire before we drop. This gives most governments a bit of a headache as the money they have to plough into our pension entitlement is reducing, at exactly the time when more is needed. This means that we can expect State pensions to be worth far less as time goes on and they may even start later. We should be preparing for this eventuality now. Being happier could just be putting in place a pension plan that offers more when it's time to hang up the boots and is not over-optimistic in terms of contributions while you are working. Most people I have spoken to over the years fall into one of two camps; either they are unconcerned about retiring and think it will sort itself out somehow; or, they have applied themselves to the task in hand. It's not like many other things we try to achieve, as it's really long-term and won't bear any fruit for some time. We can, however, monitor the position and at the end of each year assess what we have in the pot.

Retirement Myths

As well as the very nature of retirement being quite different for all of us, what steps we need to take in preparation for the big day are also individual. Martin Bamford outlines six myths in his book, *How to Retire 10 Years Early*:

'1) The State will look after me – if all you have to live on during retirement is a State pension, you will have a fairly meagre existence.
2) There is no tax to pay during retirement – we all have to pay tax when we earn money, regardless of our age.
3) My cost of living will be lower when I retire – the cost of living for retired people generally rises faster than the cost of living for people still in work.
4) My home is my pension – because you will still need a place to live during retirement, the total sale of your property is probably not an option.
5) You need a massive pension fund to retire in comfort – don't rely on generic guidelines that tell you how much you need to save for retirement. Personalise the calculations based on your own financial position and lifestyle requirements.
6) You don't need to plan for retirement because you will continue

to work – it is wrong to assume you can keep working forever.'

You may not agree with all of these points but we all have pre-conceptions about what our retirement might mean for ourself and those around us that need challenging. This is a function of our circumstances changing over time and if we start to consider this stage only a few years before we want to retire, there is only a limited amount we can change and improve.

Cost during Retirement

Like most people, I was labouring under the impression that during retirement my spending would fall dramatically. The more I researched this, the clearer it became that this assumption needed to be challenged. The biggest thing that became apparent was that I didn't actually spend much when I was working but usually lots flowed out of the wallet when I wasn't at the office. There were, of course, savings on travel and clothes, but I would probably want to eat out and holiday just as much and was hardly going to rely solely on a senior citizens bus pass. Looking at the situation, I put costs into two categories:

1) Costs which would remain the same or rise – likely to include all home-related items like heating, television, phone, etc. but also holidays, other leisure pursuits, running a car and meals out. The sandwich at my desk wasn't going to be replaced by anything less expensive and in fact I could forsee a lunchtime diet of only smoked salmon, rocket salad and a glass or two of crisp New Zealand chenin blanc taking its place!

2) Costs that would fall or stop altogether – having the mortgage and other loans paid of will certainly affect the outgoings and for many people the family-related bills should go down (although most of my friends seem to experience only a slight decline). Costs relating to getting to and from work and the odd splash on something smart might also help this side of the equation.

The conclusion from all this is definitely that some work needs to

'There are only two ways to live your life, one is as if everything is a miracle, the other is as if nothing is a miracle.' Albert Einstein

be done on reducing outgoings before our earning potential starts to fall. Otherwise, we will see savings being eaten into at a potentially alarming rate. One of the biggest advantages of starting your own venture or company is having the ability to keep revenue coming long after big corporations want to replace us with a younger model. This does depend on your business being profitable and cash positive of course.

The Real Cost of Debt

I managed to buy my first property in partnership with a good friend when we were both at university. I was bemoaning the seriously high cost of renting a flat and did some figures. Paying a mortgage seemed no greater than the rent bill each month. We pulled together a bit of money and then all we needed to do was persuade a reputable lending institution that we were fine, upstanding citizens, albeit a little younger than their usual mortgage customers. We had a couple of big things on our side and I knew it. These wonderful organisations wanted to ensnare people as early as possible and the chances of people actually moving between banks, in those days, was slim. The other factor was a general view that property was a safe investment and if we had a reasonable deposit, we should be able to convince someone to lend to us. I remember the conversation to this day; the fairly aggressive approach we took was 'if you don't want to lend to us, we'll go down the road and find someone who will', which proved successful. The lesson here is to see what is possible in the financial climate you find yourself in and then go for it.

First Step Up

Getting a foot on the property ladder was a big step forward and although I really wasn't a big fan of debt, I was able to make the distinction between positive and negative types:

Positive borrowing – covers those deals that allow us to purchase things that are more likely to go up in value and usually carry a fairly low rate of interest. Mortgages for houses obviously fall into this section but can also include some loans for essential items. We should also make the distinction here between things we need and things we want.

Negative debt – is usually expensive borrowing for goods that are going down in value. Credit and store cards are often the worst vehicles as the cost (usually expressed as APR – annual percentage rate) is high. The ease with which these companies usually lend to us never ceases to amaze me. Borrowing for a brand new car or most household goods is included in this category.

Borrowing and Saving

Here is a quick summary of some debt alternatives along with a few pointers from some of the successful people I have met. Tax relief and some specific measures vary from country to country and time to time but in recent years there has been a greater globalisation of borrowing and lending instruments as often the same financial institutions are involved. When we assess our borrowings and savings it may seem that we are only saving half a percentage point here or being charged slightly lower fees there, but this all adds up over time. Let's look at the various savings and borrowings you might make:

Standard mortgage – if you have a mortgage, take a look at the small print to see how easy it is to switch, exactly what rate you are paying and how long you have left. A good friend of mine had a big mortgage that he had taken out five or six years before but which was now looking quite expensive. He found himself in the position of being able to pay off a lump sum so I told him to call the lender and renegotiate the deal based on a term of 20 not 25 years. After a few conversations (it's rarely as simple as it should be), he now pays a little more each month but will do so for five fewer years, thereby reducing his total payments substantially. This guy can now see the light at the end of his particular tunnel: the day that he finally makes that last payment to the lender and his house becomes 100% his own.

Flexible mortgage – relatively new instrument but a great addition to the borrowing shopping basket. Flexible mortgages vary but generally offset any money in a current account against the outstanding mortgage sum. This means we only pay interest on the net amount. These deals also allow us to pay back sums early or increase the amount borrowed if you have other needs, such as an extension, refurbishment, etc. For me, flexibility is the key ingredient as our financial requirements will vary over time.

Fixed vs Variable – I'm sorry to say there is no right or wrong answer to this question. Whether you fix an interest rate or allow it to float with the bank base rate all depends on the deals on offer at the time and what best suits you as a borrower. If knowing exactly how much you have to pay each month is crucial, then a fixed interest period should be best but they are not always the cheapest in the long run. The key is to shop around and try to get two or three independent views. I like to look at this as trying to balance the short-term payments with the total amount you will pay back over the length of the mortgage or loan.

Fees – getting a new mortgage or loan can seem beneficial in terms of lending rate but they can carry hidden fees or expensive arrangement costs. It is always worth questioning everyone attached to the deal on what upfront costs are associated with your preferred course of action and then get the response in writing. The other thing to bear in mind is this is a very competitive arena and there may well be room to negotiate fees!

Government pension – for most of our working life we make payments to the Government in exchange for a pension entitlement. In the UK these payments are called National Insurance Contributions (NICs) and called by various other names in different parts. Based on the number of years and the actual amount paid, you will be entitled to a State pension starting at a retirement age set by them. If you don't know how much this is, write to the department and get a valuation. You may have the option to not pay NICs depending on your employment status so it's worth starting a direct dialogue.

Private pension – the reason we put extra money into another pension fund rather than simply keep it in a bank account is because of the tax relief. Your pension contributions should be looked after by a specialist fund manager whose job it is to put your cash into a large pension pot along with others' contributions and then invest that cash wisely for maximum return. Government rules on taking money out of a private scheme will change over time and can get more complicated every year but you should try to get some advice regularly.

Annuity – the money assembled in your pension fund after you retire can be turned into an annuity, which will provide a monthly income for the rest of your life. This can give peace of mind, if you are concerned about having a predictable income in later life.

Self-Invested Personal Pension (SIPP) – similar tax advantages apply to other pensions as for a SIPP but we have more control over how the money is invested. Again, most governments don't make it easy as regulations on what we can and cannot invest in seem to shift. For UK citizens it is currently possible to invest in commercial property, businesses ventures and companies in most parts of the world and in most sectors. It is also possible to split a fund so that a proportion is placed, for example, in Far East equities, some in government fixed interest bonds and the remainder in unlisted UK firms. Residential property is currently exempt. One thing to bear in mind is that the more diverse and complicated your spread of investments, the larger the fees you may have to pay. It is highly likely that as time marches on, there will be greater flexibility for your SIPP, should you want to exploit it.

Unsecured pension – an alternative to converting your pension into an annuity is leaving the lump sum in place and receiving income based on the interest earned. This is something that could work if you don't need the certainty of a fixed income or perhaps when annuity rates are unattractive. This is often the case in tough economic times. If you convert a lump sum to an annuity at a later date, it should provide a better annual income. Currently it's possible to do this for around ten years from the date of your retirement without suffering any tax penalty.

Individual Savings Account (ISA) – the best advice over the last 20 years for most of us is to not sink all our money into one pension scheme but spread it across a number of areas. Any money you pay into an ISA doesn't benefit from any tax relief at source but we are likely to pay less tax when we take the money out. There is an annual ceiling on the amount of money we can invest which is regularly reviewed.

Collective investing – many IFAs offer products that benefit from economies of scale. That means if we invest alone we get a certain percentage but if a group agrees to the same vehicle, returns can be greater. It's also possible to pay lower fees as they are spread over a larger pool of cash. Although these sorts of deals can be lucrative, there can be heavy costs associated with taking your money out before the maturity date. If this is attractive, try to opt for a fairly short period thereby giving yourself greater flexibility.

Investing in property – this has become an obsession for some and often seen as a way of making a fast buck! Many go into this alone but with few skills or relevant experience to make it work in the long term. If attracted to property development as a way of expanding your portfolio of investments, have a think about a partnership route or hiring the right skills at the outset. It can help overcome some of the problems along the way, especially when having two pairs of hands is better than one. Timing is key in this business as property prices and rental yields vary from year to year.

Cash – always have something tucked away, if you can, for that unexpected bill, change of circumstances or essential purchase. It's always made me sleep better at night!

'Let's live with that small pittance that we have; who coverts more, is evermore a slave.' Robert Herrick, Poet

Personal Profile – Peter

Background – runs the business that his father started and has managed to grow it substantially. It was important for his confidence and self-esteem, to have added something new or taken the company into a new phase. This guy is flamboyant and very outgoing, but has time for others, building strong bonds with people like few I have ever known.

Success – Peter considers many of us can be self-limiting! He feels our level of success is heavily restricted by the view of our immediate surroundings and often we can achieve bigger and better things by looking outside our comfort zone. We can also be limited by our own aspirations. Success for him is also about having the ability to challenge his norms and outlook regularly, pushing himself towards new achievements.

Work Balance – when we feel under pressure at work, Peter believes it is more down to the state of mind we are in. If we are able to keep striving and be aware of what is going on around us, we will soon be positive again. Recognising we will go through mental ups and downs as individuals helps him to manage the swings in his life. He also likes to see those around him adopt an employer attitude rather than that of an employee. Technology has helped him considerably in terms of making internal processes work more smoothly and efficiently but he is conscious he is much more accessible now. He works in the service sector and is often customer-facing so technology has certainly not made life (as opposed to processes) any easier as he is easily contactable and has to respond far more quickly.

Retirement – he doesn't even understand the term any more. This is something that only applies to a previous generation and not to people who are doing what they want. If he had an extra million pound in the bank, he would still work as he gains a lot of enjoyment from it; he feels it is part of him and it's what makes him perform better as a person.

Advice – if we are feeling on some kind of merry-go-round, find a way to get off! Many of us work for companies that provide a security blanket, a big office and car, a good salary, etc but we end up spending most of our life doing things that don't make us happy. This is a mental cul-de-sac.

Money Saving Tips

Most successful entrepreneurs I have known have vision and a desire to do something a bit different, but they also have an ability to cut their financial cloth according to their requirements. None of the people I interviewed was born with a silver spoon in their mouth and many recount tales when times were tough or when difficult money-related decisions had to be made. Many of those experiences have helped shape their career and attitude to their work–life balance. I'm not trying to be a miserly penny-pincher (although some might disagree!) here but here a few tips that might just help when the going gets tough:

* Drive an older car and keep it a bit longer – just get one with a bit of style.

* Get a water meter fitted.

* Renegotiate all your insurance policies every year, without compromising on coverage or security.

* Shop online to save money, where you can.

* Visit charity shops – you never know what you might find and it's a great way to give back to your community.

* Threaten to switch utility providers if you don't get a better deal.
* Never pay full price.
* Swap and barter, rather than buy.
* Take a packed lunch to work – it's going to be healthier as well.
* Walk rather than drive, where possible.
* Grow your own herbs, spices and vegetables.
* Drink tap water not the bottled variety.
* Really shop around for the best holiday price and be as flexible as you can on timing and destination.
* Ditch the home telephone and/or get one supplier to provide Internet services, mobile, telephone and your television needs.

Lifestyle Balance Sheet

Assets and liabilities can be looked at in a number of ways – any glance at a major corporation's balance sheet shows us that. It is possible, however, to apply the rules underlying this peculiar financial statement to our own lives. Just like any company, we need to have the right mix of long- and short-term borrowings, fixed assets and immediate cash. The same good practice for a healthy company or venture is not different from our own financial situation. For example, many people have invested heavily in their long-term future and bought assets like a main house, sometimes a second property, expensive bits of furniture, etc. but are now cash-strapped. Their lifestyles and amount of flexibility have been seriously affected because too much has been locked up and is not available for use. Part of creating the right balance in our lives is about having an equilibrium to our finances that is not only sensible, but also appropriate to the life we want to lead.

Final Thoughts – No Pain, No Gain

The language of finance and wealth is often as challenging as trying to get to grips with what course of action to take when it comes to pension planning. The advice given to me has consistently been to get good help and try to understand the basics at the very least. Here are a few key points from this chapter:

– Perceptions – we need to remove our natural financial preconceptions in order to be able to make good decisions.

– Action – our situation isn't going to improve on its own and enlisting professional help is essential for all of us.

– Borrowing – try to limit borrowing to assets that are more likely to appreciate, or are essential items, rather than 'nice to have'.

– Government – start or improve your direct dialogue with the various state departments that have an influence on your financial health. Tax is often the largest single cost we pay in our lives.

– Risk and reward – starting a business doesn't have to be like gambling, if you are able to change the odds.

– Retirement – requires action well in advance of the 'big day'. Give yourself as much flexibility as you can in the money being put aside and be clear about your entitlement.

– Tax allowances – try to use all your personal allowance, etc. each year to build a nest-egg.

– Trade-off – everything in your working life is negotiable including working fewer hours for less pay. To have a better work–life balance we may require some fundamental changes.

– Question of balance – try to balance your short- and longer-term financial plans to give both good returns on your money along with flexibility.

Random Mind Matter

* Preparation and the basics – I interviewed ten graphic designers for a freelance post in one of my businesses not long ago and was amazed at how little real thought and application had been put in to the preparation. I had asked them to turn up at a certain time, bring their CV and portfolio, think about a particular book project and to meet at my offices. Three forgot their CV and/or portfolio, four were either late or early and one couldn't find the office at all and had to call for help. Most had thought a bit about the project but only two had actually prepared anything. Only three people had even bothered to look at my company's website and half looked inappropriately dressed given the job was client-facing. There was only a single person who did what I considered the basics in terms of preparation and they got the job. I know this is a creative industry but in any business process, the basics can be of great value.

* Martin Bamford in *How to Retire 10 Years Early* states, 'It is estimated that, in the UK, we waste £7.9m each year by not taking

steps to reduce our tax payments.' I'm sure this applies to just about every country that systematically tries to overtax its inhabitants.

* 'Defeat is a state of mind. No-one is ever defeated until defeat has been accepted as reality. To me, defeat in anything is merely temporary, and its punishment is but an urge for me to give greater effort to achieve a goal. Defeat simply tells me that something is wrong in my doing; it is a path leading to success and truth.' Bruce Lee.

* 'Opportunity is missed by most people because it is dressed in overalls and looks like work'. Thomas Edison, founder of the electric light bulb.

* Smouldering in every boom are the flames of bust – I heard a lovely story of a very go-ahead city-type young guy who was given a shirt for Christmas, which looked the right size and suitable colour. He took one look at the label and discarded it because it wasn't a well-known brand. It's at times like this I realise we need tough times to challenge and re-balance certain perspectives.

8 The Internet and Other Revolutions

Aim

To make sense of some of the massive changes happening at the workplace, in the way we do business, even in the most basic commercial tasks. The Internet and communications revolution will continue to have a tremendous impact on consumer attitudes and buyer behaviour in profound ways affecting just about every company, commercial enterprise and worker.

'The privilege of a lifetime is being who you are.'
Joseph Campbell

N et Phases

The generally accepted wisdom is there have been three phases in the Internet revolution:

Phase 1 – 1990s to 2000: Computing left the desktop bound for the world wide web; companies set up all over the place promising huge potential and profits from this shift. Potential seemed more real than profits, at the time, as commercial activity lagged behind technological developments. Websites, portals, search engines and other fancy things sprang up, seemingly on a daily basis, until the bubble burst. Computer usage and Internet penetration grew dramatically but many new ventures went down in flames because of set up and marketing costs. It was a period of trial and error, but there was an overriding sense there was more to come.

Phase 2 – 2000 to 2008: The whole notion of whether we would buy things on the Internet was laid to rest, once and for all as e-commerce grew exponentially year on year in just about every field. From holidays to clothes and cars to CDs, we would now buy in increasingly large numbers without leaving the comfort of our own home. This has, and will continue to have, an acute impact on the look of our high streets and how towns and cities develop. Personal interaction has also been completely redefined, with a whole generation now meeting in virtual space rather than face-to-face. The amount of times we meet online and communicate using computers, mobiles and other devices with friends, family and work colleagues has exploded beyond belief. YouTube, Google, Facebook, Twitter, Cyworld and many others are integral parts of many lives.

Phase 3 – 2008 and beyond: The world of wireless access, true broadband speed, video chatting, audio messaging, mobile surfing and ease of e-tailing is with us. More and more businesses will see the virtues of not just being on the web, but trading, communicating and marketing their products and services via this medium. The web is being transformed into something that is faster, slicker, more enjoyable, intuitive and compelling. There will be greater personalisation of the Internet in the same way we adapt our homes and we will have virtual lives in a virtual world running in parallel with our actual human experiences. Korea is one of the most advanced countries in the world in terms of computer usage, broadband and online social interaction. A networking site called

'Cyworld' has been incredibly popular there and allows users to create a 3D model of themself, interact in a virtual world and buy items to decorate their virtual home.

Personal Profile – James

Background – learnt the basics of business in a retail environment selling entertainment products before moving into feature film marketing and distribution. He is highly energetic and driven and now has his own company after spending many years with a Hollywood film studio.

Success – James came to a crossroads in his career when he was made redundant in his late thirties. He went to many interviews and soon came to the conclusion he didn't like the idea of being a small cog in a big wheel. He required more control over his own destiny and a change from the traditional corporate lifestyle. For a number of years he hadn't been adding the sort of value that he was capable of and wanted to test himself fully. Part of this process was looking at the gaps in his knowledge and he found the process stimulating and rewarding. Starting a company from scratch meant the future was far from certain but what gave him confidence was sticking to the clear vision he had from the outset. Having a 'proper' job does put a comfort blanket around all of us and we can easily get sucked into the world where we expect things to happen without much independent thought or effort. Running his business is completely different. A yardstick for success is confidence and he tries to remain positive at all times. Success can also be measured in the quality and effectiveness of his work relationships; if they are strong, many problems and issues can be quickly resolved. Part of achieving success is having the ability to spot when the time is right to make a change in ourself or evaluate what people we are working with. If we notice too late, the opportunity may have gone and it can take some time before it comes round again.

Work Balance – James feels that a good business life is

having a stimulating environment, one which maintains momentum and includes constructive conflict in order to achieve consistent results. How we allow technology to influence our life should be looked at, because even though it helps us respond to the ups and downs of business much more quickly, it is another key part of the work–life jigsaw that needs really good management. If all forms of inward and outbound communication can be handled properly, they will have a positive impact on the way we run our lives.

Retirement – James doesn't see the traditional retirement age as being a time for huge change. There is likely to be a slowing in pace but very much a continuation of what business tasks he enjoys.

Advice – he has always enjoyed following his own instincts and if we enjoy something, we are likely to do it better. We should always be on the lookout for new opportunities, so we can test our own skills and aims. James feels it is easy to underestimate the value of a strong network of trusted colleagues in business, which can help in achieving goals and evaluating different ways of doing things. Most people he has met enjoy doing a range of small things rather than one large task, so being able to break business down into bite-sized pieces can, in itself, add to our feeling of reward and fulfillment.

Small World

The Internet has certainly shrunk the globe and made it possible to reach huge audiences very quickly. Many companies, however, think that the net will instantly solve their business issues when, in fact, it is more important than ever to get the fundamental business principles and core values right. This technology is simply a new means of reaching people and the focus on the customer must remain at the forefront of all actions. The net provides innovators and early adopters with a chance to progress, not just on the quality of their product or service but on the excellence of their creative expression. It's an opportunity to get noticed and talked about in chatrooms, forums and networking sites. without spending vast sums on marketing or advertising.

Keeping Up

There is a big generational gap or at least a two-tier business society. Many decision-makers are not keeping pace with the Internet revolution which is providing those who do with a real opportunity to get ahead. There has been a noticeable narrowing of the cultural divisions between nations as more consumers see the same products and services online at the same point in time. Consumers surfing in the west are just as likely to be buying, bidding, selling or renting in the identical space as their counterparts in the east and so on.

Internet Update

We fall into different categories when it comes to the net. There are those who have tried to ignore it, some who have reluctantly accepted its impact on their business life, and others who have embraced its existence wholeheartedly. There is a final group, however, who have completely re-examined their entire business proposition and ways of working. Not all areas of commercial activity have been affected to a huge extent but few have escaped entirely. The net can be seen as a tremendous opportunity but as many traditional and lumbering retailers have found, it can also be a major threat. The Internet has ignored the scale of business: it doesn't care whether a brand has been established for a hundred years or one. It's as if products and services have a second life, a new start, an existence that has little respect for what has gone on before. What matters to online customers is the quality of the virtual offering and experience today and that is what businesses need to address.

'We are going to put a computer on every desk and one in every home.'
Bill Gates

Last Orders

A small Scottish brewery called Brewdog was struggling to get established in the hard to penetrate world of British pubs and clubs. It decided to look at the net and the international potential that might exist for its beer. They soon saw that social networking sites, forums, chatrooms and blogging were an effective and inexpensive way of spreading their message. They identified a number of key influencers and sent out free samples. The company also decided to create videos of people talking about their products and the benefits of independent brewing. It took some time but business slowly picked up and orders started flowing in from all over the world. Without the Internet, Brewdog would have had to use traditional ways of selling and marketing their beers and, like many small, regional brewers, it was likely they would be pushed out of business by the big guys who offer better prices and marketing support. The net has given this inventive company a real place in the market; an opportunity to fight on their own terms, and a better chance of success.

This is a Religion

As an indication of the impact of the Internet, just take a look at the Pope's channel (yes, channel!) on YouTube. Even one of the most traditional and conservative organisations like the Catholic Church is harnessing the power of online social networking to spread its message and garner support.

Politics on the Net

Barack Obama was certainly the first American President and possibly the first leading politician to extensively use the power of the web to help get elected. Take a look at obama.com. It was one of the core foundations of his communication strategy and with it he managed to deliver his message to a broader and wider audience, affecting the voting of many who don't attend political rallies. It has video and audio, a place to donate, a good blog area, a place to buy his merchandise and add your comments. Then there's the other places you can find his messages including Facebook, MySpace, YouTube, Flickr, Twitter, Eventful, LinkedIn and the list goes on. This was about getting into places where traditional politicians have feared to tread. He has moved the goalposts in political campaigning and set a new benchmark for others round the world.

Web Partners

It is now possible to build a fully functioning web business that combines Google's skills and your own vision. Google is one of the greatest brands on the net (in fact anywhere!) and it has an impressive record of thinking ahead of its competitors and often customers. Many big companies look at the establishment of large business partnerships with some scepticism, perhaps because they feel they would have too many eggs in one basket. For small companies, sole operators or fledgling ventures, the approach needs to be different. We can usually only manage a certain number of relationships at the same time and therefore need to develop business links which bring more than one benefit, if possible. Google has understood this and is no longer just a search engine, it is also a payment processing platform, an advertising agency, a research tool and a way to reach new audiences. It is possible to build a business proposition using Google skills along with our own vision and very few others. Many successful businessmen have understood the importance in using talents of partner companies to help their own proposition flourish and it has never been more important than today. There needs to be trust and the ability to find partners that are in it for the long haul but areas may be left unexploited without such deals. I heard a saying a while back which still applies to relationships where there is something to lose by another's errors: 'If you don't trust them completely, don't work with them'.

Build a Community

Creating online communities, forums, blogs, etc. can seem to many companies a luxury rather than a must-have part of their communication strategy or marketing effort. Traditional marketing mailshots, advertising campaigns and expensive brochures do have a lovely tangibility but are increasingly less powerful than online engagement, and usually more expensive. As an example, I have done quite a lot of work with one large international glass company who has needed to establish themselves on the web in order to help spread their message to new customers. They have a lot of technical information, which is important for any company that owns a building with any sort of glass usage over and above straightforward windows. Government regulations are now very tight on how often glass structures need examination and how they can be fixed to the basic infrastructure of buildings. I have been trying to encourage this company to start a blog and create a series of notice-boards and forums on technical issues to help others and show off their expertise. It has been an uphill struggle. It needs a new breed of businessperson; someone who can see how this strategy is a better way of getting closer to customers than sending them a glossy brochure every now and again. They would be the first in their sector to do it and it would put them ahead of their competitors.

Wrong Can Be Right

Keywords are vital to any website that depends (even in part) on people searching for the product or service they are selling. Invisible key words (or meta-tags) are embedded in the site code so that the search engines can find and rank that location. I came across some code the other day, which amused me as it was for a company that had a name which could easily be misspelled. They had included many of the common misspellings in their key meta-tags, so that if a potential user didn't quite put the correct spelling into a search engine, they would still find them. This is the sort of thinking that can really drive traffic and open new opportunities.

Search Engine Optimisation (SEO)

SEO is one of the fastest growing areas of the online world and the commercial rewards for high ranking are immense. For example, if a business doesn't get listed on the first page of your chosen search engine, they will miss out on 97% of customers. That means only 3% of searchers connect with anyone on subsequent pages. Many companies still look to buy ads in the hope they get the click-through but this can be expensive. The alternative way of looking at this is to build strong recognition in niche areas and grow from that point. If you are able to target small clusters of consumers where you can definitely make the first page on a search engine, you will not only get people to your site, but will do it at lower cost. Having this traffic will have the secondary benefit of potentially increasing the ranking for other pages or promotional initiatives as well.

Look and Feel

Many sites are created by individuals who understand the technology and who can write html, xml, java, flash or a bunch of other fast-developing software. Few of those, however, understand the aesthetics of what they are trying to achieve. Creating an emotionally stimulating and absorbing experience online is not only about how slick the code works or what bells and whistles it has. It's also about visualisation because of the impact on user behaviour and that's why creating a website is often best approached as a team task rather than by a single individual. Some propositions can be successful without having to look elegant but the point is whether they would have been more so, if they conveyed an understanding of what users like to see. Website development, especially homepage design, is now more akin to magazine or newspaper publishing. If consumers don't like or engage with the look of something, they will simply go somewhere else: it's a bit like channel hopping on our television sets. In exactly the same way as a written advert that contains too many words can turn people off, a website with too much content will not get past first base with many potential customers. If you are thinking about creating a new site from scratch or feel like a change to your existing site would be beneficial, have separate meetings with coders and graphic designers. The best solution must be to use Internet technology to the fullest making sure you are appealing to customers and being search-engine-friendly at the same time. If your website hasn't changed much in the last six months, it's time to have a rethink.

Participation

Why should people come back to your site? Do you have the most competitive pricing, useful information or best service? Most of us can't compete with big companies on price, fulfillment or other things, but we can offer a more personal experience. The vast majority of success stories on the web are those who offer a very specialist product or service. Providing others a place to have their say, make a comment and interact with other like-minded individuals will bring reward. Getting people to return to a site regularly is all about emotional attachment – wanting to meet your online friends, add comments, get help or just see what is going on. In many areas of business, this means a good chatroom, good product info pages, a frequently updated notice board, blogs and/or a forum. Once a customer base is built, there are opportunities to sell, generate advertising revenue and exploit co-marketing deals. I have seen many small web ventures fail, however, because after some initial success, they stop offering new ideas and experiences. This results in people losing interest in the site and returners stop returning and surfers quickly move on. Before you know it, other people's chatrooms are bouncing with discussions of sites that have cool content.

Mum's the Word

I have keenly followed the progress of mumsnet.com since its inception. It has an immediate impact with a catchy tagline ('by parents for parents') and places emphasis on reviewing new products for safety, quality, value for money, etc. It has lots of offers, competitions, a place to personalise your visit and a newsletter that is well written. On just about every visit, I am impressed at the amount of new content, new discussion points, discounts and how easy it is to navigate. It seems to focus on combining useful information with a specialist place to browse for the items users are looking for and this is a strategy that clearly works.

Website Checklist

Here is a quick and easy checklist for developing, expanding or building a website:

1) Engagement – start by writing the key messages you want someone to read first. It's the equivalent of the lead stories of a newspaper or feature articles in a magazine.

2) Content – before starting to look at different design ideas get all your content in a pot. This should include text for the launch and new wording for several months, images and replacements, quotes, reviews, offers, competitions, links, etc.

3) Site map – build a diagram on a single piece of paper with a box for each separate page on the site. Everything will flow from the homepage but where do you want users to go after that?

4) Partners – who will be your e-commerce partners? Fulfillment house, key suppliers, technical back-up, etc.

5) Links – try to get as many inbound and outbound links as possible, no matter how seemingly unrelated they might appear. It helps

your SEO.

6) Co-marketing – there are lots of others out there who may be open to co-promotions and joint deals. Offering a discount on their products can be a user benefit for your site and vice versa. Providing advertising space on your site with a reciprocal arrangement can only help both parties.

7) Loading times – ensure your site doesn't take, even the slowest computer, too long to load. This means making sure images, audio files or video clips are not too large.

8) Click rate – keep the number of clicks required to get to a purchase or desired key action to a minimum.

9) Database – gather a database of users whenever possible by offering good incentives such as a newsletter, exclusive deals, some unique content, an online event, etc.

10) Technology – your website needs to look good and be robust but does not need to include all the latest (and often expensive) tricks. The key question is whether new technology will significantly improve the customer proposition or ultimately, increase revenue.

11) Personal – keep the offers, advice, editorial, etc. personal and real. No one likes jargon or slick corporate-speak.

12) Viral marketing – every message you emit, via email or other means, could carry a reason for someone to come to your site. Tempt potential visitors with something intriguing or different.

13) Encourage a direct connection – try to get users to email their views and ideas, both positive and negative – with permission you can even then include them on the site somewhere which helps with the turnover of new and interesting information.

14) Network – piggy-back existing online networks and events.

15) Stats – track traffic stats to identify which browsers people are using and what days or times of the day attract the most hits. Your Internet Service Provider (ISP) should be able to help or Google Analytics offers a good service.

Personal Profile – Louise

Background – innovative life coach and trainer, Louise has worked with businesses of all shapes and sizes over the years but gets the most reward from one-to-one work. She started her own business several years ago to have greater control over what she teaches and when she operates.

Success – success is about being more self-aware in order to identify the important areas of life. This enables her to prioritise daily tasks while moving in the right direction. She believes when we get out of balance, we are often trying to be someone we are not and recognising who that illusionary figure is, can be a great help. When feeling out of balance, she tries to identify a time in her life when she was in balance. Finally, if we don't follow our passions and emotions closely we can get out of balance very quickly.

Work Balance – she has been having great fun listening to Deepak Chopra talk about health and quantum physics lately, and has been very interested in one of the areas that he talks about: heart disease. According to the Department of Health Education and Welfare Institute in the USA, it was discovered that the major risk factors leading to heart disease are: smoking, hypertension or high cholesterol. The majority of people studied, in fact, also had the following two risk factors for this illness: low self-happiness and low job satisfaction. They discovered more people died of heart disease at 9am on a Monday morning than at any other time. We all perceive our lives and the world we live in with the thoughts and feelings that we believe are true and real for us. However, consider that you are creating your reality with the thoughts and feelings that you are running at this exact moment. If you are running thoughts and feelings that are about unhappiness and dissatisfaction, then these have consequences in your body. We go to work in a field of energy that exists within us and around us that is linked to our thoughts and feelings. Therefore, it would seem like a powerful step towards achieving great health to work on our thoughts and feelings.

Advice – how often do you laugh? Think about what it feels and sounds like to have a good laugh – it's rather different to clenching your body tightly with stress and anxiety. Follow what you love in life and make choices based upon following what will create more love, passion, joy and better health in your life.

Simple Items Can Work

I read an article about a guy who sold vacuum cleaner bags. Nathan Wood started in 2002 in a city in the middle of Britain and because of the upheaval on the high street (shops closing, rent rises, etc), he started a website to improve and grow the business. I visited the site (dustbag.co.uk) and when was certainly far from state of the art or aesthetically pleasing but it did do the basics. He eventually closed his high street shop and now only operates on the web putting plenty of thought and effort into maximising his traffic. I Googled three separate words and his website came out on the first page each time. Wood had used Google's AdWords service as a promotional platform but also local search facilities and directories to boost customer awareness. Offering something different on the web and understanding how best to increase business can certainly reap big rewards.

Two Chicks

Alla Chapples and Anna Richey set up a company called Two Chicks, which sells cartons of liquid egg whites in some of the UK high-street food retail outlets. They had no background in food, little commercial experience and bravely launched in the middle of a recession. The website is twochicks.co.uk and is informative and user-friendly. It has lots of good health tips, recipes and tells the customer where their product is stocked. With a simple idea, two people got up and made something happen and built a good business in a very short time. The Internet was a key facilitator in this.

Car e-Commerce

Many car companies have tiptoed into the world of the Internet, slowly and often with a great deal of caution. Fiat's first major foray at the end of 2008, was quite typical of many. It launched a limited edition version of its Fiat 500 in collaboration with the iconic fashion label, Diesel and it created an interactive online facility to run alongside. The site allows users to change the colour of the car, see different interiors, put stickers on the outside and add options like special hi-fi or climate control. All the time the price keeps ticking up in the corner, which although alarming if you go too mad, is actually is very reassuring as you keep track of the cost. The site uses technology in just about as basic a way a possible, with no video experience of what the car was like to drive, no audio reviews and no emotional attachment of any kind. It was like driving to the Grand Canyon and stopping to look at a hill on the way! Achieving something forthwhile needs to embrace technology fully and be empathetic with how users want to interact.

Business Online Networking

There has been a great deal of buzz about social networking sites for many years, a trend that has also affected the business community. LinkedIn (linkedin.com) is a good example of a network specifically set up for professionals that has now expanded its footprint by offering an international flavour. It recently established a French language version, aiming to reach 8% of French professionals in its first couple of years and has already signed up major companies like Renault and France Telecom. Looking for partners overseas and discussing potential for international collaboration has never been easier. The downside with all these sites is the sheer time required to build networks, maintain them, track messages and communicate with lots of people with differing aims. I have worked with many successful businesspeople who have used online networking to help grow their commercial activities in a huge variety of ways but they all talk about the ability to keep focused on the major commercial issues as a primary goal.

Blog to the Bank

For many professionals, blogging was seen for a long time as the domain of geeky teenagers and crackpot enthusiasts who don't get out enough, but many companies are now recognising it as the invaluable business tool it is. There are an estimated 40,000 new blogs started each day and although many just cover the habits of some spotty youth, the largest area of growth is in the world of business. Benefits of blogging can certainly include profile building which is a great source of customer feedback, and free software is available on the web. If you get into this activity, however, bank on technical issues as this is evolving technology and there are those out there who get a kick out of posting rubbish. However, this can be a cheap form of advertising and market research but also with potential benefits of customer loyalty.

Sites of Interest

Here are a few sites that may provide some interesting feedback:
1) adverblog.com – get ideas about digital marketing campaigns.
2) coolinfographics.blogspot.com – make information look interesting.
3) getanewbrowser.com – new things happening on the Internet.
4) marketingpathway.com – marketers post about marketing advice, tips and ideas.
5) dailymarketingace.com – Internet marketing information.
6) roadtomarketingrelevance.com – direct marketing experiences and tips.
7) smallbusiness.co.uk/blogs/ – more of a blog portal but always some interesting stuff here.
8) goodmanjones.net – accounting and financial advice.
9) allbusiness.com/bloggers/ – new business ideas and a variety of commercial topics.
10) entrepreneur.com – lots of practical thoughts and suggestions on everything from starting your own business to sales, marketing and technology.

Culture Shock

Unilever is a global brands business that owns highly visible names like Flora, SlimFast, Hellman's, Lipton, Dove, Sunsilk and Surf. I have followed its progress into digital marketing since 2007 when it won an award for its 'Dove Evolution' promotional campaign. Many businesses of this size and international stature continue to pay lip service to these kinds of messages, remaining focused on pumping out traditional advertising campaigns that are getting increasingly less productive. Unilever has received considerable exposure for its efforts to date. Take a Look!

What is Viral?

Many companies develop an online marketing campaign or series of email marketing messages then suddenly see themselves as viral gurus. The first thing is that most of the activity isn't actually viral at all. Viral is when a message or communication is spread not by the originator but by users and is about consumers sharing their experiences by telling friends and colleagues. This means any potential viral communication needs a compelling or new perspective, to offer useful advice or be written in a way that is irreverent and/or extremely witty. It should be focused to hit the target audience full in the face and can be made in video or audio, with images or just text. Location of the message needs to follow the same criteria as other web campaigns, i.e. appear on messageboards, networking sites, blogs, etc. that get a lot of traffic from the particular audience you want to hit and ideally be respected by those same people. If it isn't part of your marketing mix, it could be potentially the most effective medium.

Brick Walls

The revolution in communications, customer expectations and buyer behaviour has resulted in us having to examine the barriers to innovation and new thinking both online and offline. Here is a quick checklist that has come out of meeting people who have started ventures from scratch:

1) Start-up cash – do you have enough resources to make a prototype, prove your product works or show how a marketing campaign can reap rewards? If not, you need to get creative. This may take the form of offering shares to those people or firms who can help, negotiating part-payment in exchange for a stake of the upside or helping others in exchange for their assistance. It might be as simple as using someone else's server, e-commerce platform or online marketing knowledge but lowering initial funding requirements will help keep many avenues open.

2) Organisation and systems – most new ideas need fresh and different ways of working to enable the basic concept to flourish. Not all the answers will be immediately available because you are entering the unknown. All the scenario planning in the world will not be as useful as making those first few steps. Also try to find some people who are good with the aspects of technology that you lack experience in and start a dialogue.

3) Conviction – even really good ideas test our mental resolve and levels of self-confidence. I have always found support from those

closest to us can help when nothing seems to go right. Somehow, somewhere that inner strength has to show not just in your actions but to others as well. If you have doubts, you'll soon see that others are reserved as well.

4) Marketing – the whole world of advertising, promotions, marketing campaigns and reaching consumer groups has been turned upside down by new technology. If you have an innovative concept or new way of exploiting a need, the best way to highlight it is via a creative communications plan. Everything you do needs to be unique and echo your positioning. Don't just do the same old things or follow others.

5) Technology – you don't need to be a complete boffin about the technical aspects of your business but do need to understand the key parts of the chain: the things that can ultimately affect the way your idea gets brought to the customers and many of these will involve technology.

6) People – not having the right people supporting you can hold back even the most brilliant entrepreneur. I have always found that having a couple of good friends to chat through problems and issues with has put me in a better position to tackle whatever comes along. Try to surround yourself with good people and then liberate them.

In his book, *Futurize Your Enterprise,* **David Siegel has this to say, 'A management-led company relies on management's vision to set the course. A customer-led company is completely aligned with customer groups, both internally and externally. A customer-led company encourages conversation between customers and employees, and among customers. Rather than shying away from personal contact, a customer-led company actually encourages contact with the employees and facilitates customers meeting each other. This new emphasis on listening creates the conversations that move the company forward'.**

Seen Nothing Yet

The Internet has changed the fundamentals of how many of us do business, where we buy products and how we spend our time. The next ten years will see an even more profound shift in consumer behaviour requiring businesses to have an even sharper focus on quality of offering, a far more holistic approach to marketing and selling plus a completely new relationship with potential customers. Most of us will have to re-think the structure of our organisations, how we work with others and what partnering really means, if we are to stay ahead of the game.

Online Vision

Almost every day I see another business viewing the web as a trade show, shop front or online catalogue, and the rough ride is just about to start for those poor souls. Trying to offer everything to everyone is a sure way to fall further behind and instead of customer satisfaction going up, it can go in the opposite direction. Having worked with a large distribution business for some time, we met up to discuss their website as the main sales guys didn't seem very enthusiastic. It turned out a member of their IT department had built the site and the online marketing initiatives had absolutely nothing to do with the sales department. Far from being a single outward-facing online business, this was about a few people wanting to emit a whole series of messages that had little to do with the rest of the company via a customer-facing website.

I challenged the lot of them to sit back and take a cold, hard look at their presence on the web, their online marketing and how new products and services were introduced into the ether. For many companies, their website is a reflection of their organisation chart, which are rarely easy to use or offer an intuitive customer experience. Many people are still looking at the online world as a way of putting a few products and/or services into some kind of virtual car park, which is difficult to get into, poorly designed and which you are always glad to leave.

Personal Profile – Tony

Background – worked for the BBC in special effects after completing an electronics degree, before moving into film and video editing. His motivation came from trying to find something he really enjoyed rather than looking for the best-paid career. After some good years and progress, he set up a company with a colleague but this did not work out for either of them. This gave him the impetus to do something he had always wanted to and took a year out to build himself a house. This had the added advantage of giving him the space to assess where he wanted his career to go, while being fully removed from it. Tony is very much an early adopter.

Success – he believes success has a material dimension, although cash is simply a means to an end. Many of us get too carried away with the accumulation of wealth rather than having the lifestyle that we either want or need. Having the flexibility to work the hours he wants, in the manner he wants, is a big part of personal success. We should try to reward ourselves for doing tasks to the best of our ability and get real satisfaction from that, but often the very pace of our lives makes this difficult. Maintaining a healthy lifestyle is definitely a reflection of success as well as having time to explore new technologies and ideas.

Work Balance – most of his working life has been as a freelancer and it is easy to become a workaholic because of how difficult it is to turn work away. He made the decision to maintain social engagements, so it was easier to keep a perspective on what was happening around him.

Technological changes have been a double-edged sword, it has enabled many people to edit video themselves on their computer, forcing down rates in his business, but he can now complete projects far more quickly. Keeping pace with change is something he very much enjoys and benefits from having a strong network of friends, who frequently share information and experiences. He believes that being protective of information, ideas, etc. is very short-sighted. Constantly looking at new features and software to enable him to offer a dynamic and competitive service can absorb a lot of time but he tries to look at areas he finds interesting. Tony also believes security in our chosen career is now about skill base and feels that working for large corporations can, in fact, erode our talents. This is because few big companies adopt change at the same rate as smaller ones. We can become too mentally and physically comfortable and that means we stop learning at the same rate, and making us most at risk.

Retirement – Tony is not entirely sure what retirement will mean or what he would like it to be. Certainly spending more time with friends, travelling and developing hobbies is attractive but he also likes the rewards of being productive and making money as well. He poses the question that if we spent all the time on holiday, would it feel like a holiday? Perhaps we need to continue working, even in small ways, to ensure we get enough mental stimulation to keep the balance even in retirement.

Advice – he has seen many people jump from full time occupation to no work and it usually doesn't make for a happy transition. Trying to scale back in a logical fashion is definitely what he will be trying to do.

Customer Requirements

An outward-looking website's starting point is what the customer is looking for; what information they require and what experience will they enjoy. This is easier said than done, however, due to the differing attitudes to online usage. Confident Internet users instantly know what they are looking for and how to find it, while others need more hand-holding and explanation from the landing page onwards. Users must be effortlessly guided from page to page and led in the same way that magazines encourage us to turn to the next page of an article or feature. This is diametrically opposite to starting with the company mission statement and hoping that a customer will email you for further help. Poorly constructed websites are e-rubbish.

E-commerce to e-trading

E-commerce to e-trading
I find it difficult to remember Dell having a traditional offline business, such is the ease and enthusiasm with which it has embraced the Internet. Their entire site is a great example of how to be customer-focused as it looks at user needs first and foremost, and doesn't just list products and services. This open philosophy continues on each page and avoids the hard sell. Designated places to obtain technical feedback, ask questions and see experiences of other customers, all add to the feeling this is a good and helpful place to be. The culture seems to be that their website is far from being just another division or part of their business, but it is their entire means of communicating. Their ability to make the transition from e-commerce to e-trading, has meant their market share has grown considerably compared to its competitors, many of whom are still in the online starting-blocks.

Online Loyalty

Online Loyalty
Many businesses I have worked with, both large and small, take their existing contact with customers to the Internet and expect that relationship to be the same. The loyalty they have built is expected to transfer seamlessly online because a nice-looking website has suddenly sprung up. Emotional attachment does not exist in the online world in the same way as it does elsewhere. Many people now use price comparison sites to check offers and conditions before they purchase and they check reviews before purchasing. If they can purchase something cheaper from a different source, there is a strong possibility they will buy providing the website proposition is a good one. Many big name brands thought their brand alone would make them successful on the net but they hadn't really appreciated that customer loyalty is shrinking as the traditional business model alters. Let's take a big-name clothes brand; it used to be able to dictate a front of store location and plenty of staff available to offer assistance. People who buy online can now seek similar goods at a cheaper price with just a few clicks. Part of the value in the brand was seeing the goods in the store but now fewer people visit those places and are content to be in a virtual shopping environment. Unless that brand can give a similar experience to these new e-shoppers, their revenue is likely to drop considerably.

Price Mechanism

If you are having a tough time pricing your product or service because of the ease with which customers can now compare, you may need to change the price mechanism. If you don't want to compete on cost, don't! Offer combinations of products, limited editions, special offers (not just 10% off) and the option for consumers to tailor-make. I have seen many book publishers put their catalogue of titles onto a website and hope they will sell. Few engage the reader or offer anything different. Amazon, on the other hand, remains very active at responding to what we are looking for or wish to purchased.

**'The number one benefit of information technology is that it empowers people to do what they want to do. It lets people be creative. It lets people be productive. It lets people learn things they didn't think they could learn before, and so in a sense it is all about potential.'
Steve Ballmer, CEO Microsoft**

Tips from Net-Smart People

During my research, I have met a lot of people who have applied themselves, often because of immense fascination, to the world of the Internet and other related technological changes. Most have seen new trends coming before the rest of us, spotting how to use new applications or taking new ideas and fusing them together to add value. Here are some tips from my experiences in this area:
* Get rid of the old – not a doctrine for euthanasia but an under-standing that in order to implant new ideas into people's day-to-day working lives, we have to remove some of what is currently in the way. As an example, voicemail is too laborious and filing cabinets are a relic from the past.
* Help culture – we don't all adopt new concepts at an identical

rate and in the same way, so developing a culture that gets early adopters to help others can lift a whole business. Even though someone might be slow at the start, it is not to say that person won't come up with something earth-shattering which helps everyone later.
* email hell – how much time is spent reading unnecessary emails? Someone has got to stand up and make an example of those who 'cc' too many people. Otherwise we will all get bogged down in email mire.
* e-library – many companies have an online store or back-up which keeps a log of emails, etc. and other useful documents. It rarely includes things, however, which haven't been digital, useful marketing pictures, press releases, competitor brochures or a series of old ads. Having an immediately accessible library of interesting and relevant items can help the innovation process and ensure that some topics don't get forgotten too early. It is like building your own, bespoke and highly specific wikipedia. Something that people are encouraged to contribute to and use.
* Internet openness – flag interesting, innovative and relevant things on the web and get people internally to review the best and worst features.
* Evaluate everything – many companies will be constantly trying to find the latest things on the Internet and if you can review and evaluate as many as possible, you will not be left behind. This isn't trying to create geek's corner, just to avoiding the surprise when a customer says, 'have you seen this?'. This applies to new software, applications, online advertising and e-marketing.

E-tailing

Any individual with a good idea now has the ability to chip away at established retail giants through Internet exposure and focused online marketing. In the past, there have been significant barriers to entry in retailing as launching new stores was hugely expensive. Now, for as little as a few hundred pounds, dollars, yen or euros, anyone can start a competitive e-shop. The ones that are doing well often have a core competence and detailed knowledge of a niche customer group. This makes marketing much more productive and offers something that many large players seem to struggle with, such as meaningful contact and up-to-date information. I would really like to own or work in a retail business right now, either traditional or online, as it offers a spectacular challenge. With the second phase of e-tailing in its infancy, many of the global web-based sellers will need to re-think what they are offering and how. The rise of the small, independent specialist is coming. Large e-tailers are no longer the hunters: they are the hunted!

The e-customer

If you want to have a successful web business or improve your existing online offering, there is a process that I have seen work for others. It comes from examining a number of highly successful web-centric firms to see how their evolution has developed. A summary is as follows:

1) Who – what role are you personally going to play and who else will be assigned key tasks in the online development? There needs to be a high degree of flexibility so that others can absorb new areas, otherwise things that need attention will fall through the gaps (the it's-not-my-job syndrome!).

2) Paths and goals – this is as much a description of how you want to move forward as where you expect to be. A key problem many companies find is that halfway through a big online project, the goalposts seem to have moved. This can throw everyone into chaos and it's like starting all over again. If you can keep time-frames short, it will help incorporate your changing web landscape into future stages of development.

3) Key customers – many websites try to appeal to a broad market audience. There is a saying in web-land, which is 'go deep, not broad' and it's as true today as the first time I heard it. If you can capture key customer groups, one at a time if needs be, your business will grow in the right way.

4) Listen and learn – having a business online is like watching a patient sleeping; you can't see much but you can hear the heart-beat. With the web, it's about listening to where that beat is taking you and learning every step of the way.

5) Evaluate and revise – when you get to the end of one short phase, review the process, people, successes and failures, then start all over again. The cycles of development happen too quickly to be able to stop to admire your handiwork.

A ge of Innovation

We are entering, or perhaps are already in, the age of innovation. This is a period far removed from the agricultural age, the industrial revolution or most recently the consumer spending bonanza. It is a phase of our workplace evolution that is as profound as moving from the fields to the factory floor and will affect us all. The consumer spending era gave rise to information being of paramount importance. The people who reacted swiftest and took the time to understand the data available, often collected a pot of gold. As the Internet has matured it has meant knowledge is virtually ubiquitous and immediately accessible. This has resulted in new skills being required to succeed.

What we now need to do is to embrace a process of re-thinking our business proposition, re-designing our delivery, revisiting our relationship with the customer and continually moving our goalposts to keep pace with changing business demands. Value will be added in originality and innovation, aesthetics and novelty, imagination and freshness. We are all exposed to far more media than ever before, on television, newspapers, magazines and over the Internet and soon switch off when things look samey and out of date. I followed with some interest as McDonald's moved from the garish yellow and red frontage to a softer and altogether more calming colour scheme, trying to position itself as a more relaxed and supposedly environmentally friendly chain.

Touchy Feely: Ask yourself these questions:

1) Can a computer make your job or business proposition obsolete?
2) Can competitors somewhere else in the world do what you do cheaper?
3) Is your quality, delivery and service really good?
4) Do you work within a culture of continual change, being able to react to shifting consumer requirements?

Many businesses I have worked with are built on sound commercial ideals but this may not be enough as we move forward into the age of innovation. There will be a growing need to craft something different; to tailor products and services towards an emotional and more personal purchase. Consumers want individualism and we need to respond by offering bespoke solutions that do not just give a basic item but offer a unique aspect. I was a member of a bar and casino establishment for a number of years and they had image recognition software system installed. It meant whoever was on the front desk had my name flashing up on their screens when I walked through the outer doors. It made the simple experience of signing in seem like you were meeting an old friend. I would watch people come in and be greeted with a warm personal welcome, marvelling at how effective it was. I don't know how much this piece of kit cost to install but I would have thought it paid for itself many times over. Even if this kind of technology isn't applicable to your business circumstances, the concept of enhancing the customer welcome in some way probably is.

Final Thoughts – Making Connections

The impact of the Internet and other technology-fuelled changes on our career and working aspirations is profound. The sooner we are able to embrace these revolutions and the impact they are having on every part of our working life, the better equipped we will be to find the balance we strive. Anyone who thinks that what we have seen so far is the tail end of meteoric transformation, could be very disappointed. We are only at the beginning of how these developments will affect our jobs, the companies we work for and the structure of the businesses we know. Here are some of the important points from this chapter:

– Re-think – the Internet has given us the opportunity to re-evaluate the fundamentals of the business we are in and how we are going to do our job.

– Partners – we should consider the need for new partners and often those that can add significant technological benefits to our product, service, delivery or pricing.

– Marketing – what we have done before will not necessarily work in this new world, so we need to embrace what the Internet can provide including building online communities, viral campaigns, creating forums and other ways for potential customers to interact.

– Re-invent – technology and consumer requirements are moving fast and will continue to shift so we need to keep pace and never stand still.

– Engage – if we don't emotionally engage and re-engage with consumers online, we will lose them.

– Sitting comfortably – there are much smaller barriers to entry in most businesses so no-one can sit comfortably expecting their market position to go unchallenged.

– Website – most companies still don't have a site that is customer-led or aesthetically pleasing.

– Loyalty – we must expect and respond to reducing levels of customer loyalty as more products and services become fully available on the net.

Random Mind Matter

* 'In the next ten years, half of current management in the UK will retire. This large band of people constitutes the demographic known as the 'baby boomers' (born prior to 1960), whose experience of the working world is what we would now call traditional – nine-to-five and five day weeks, long-term commitment to a single organisation and a gradual working up through the corporate hierarchy. Their departure will signal the influx of Generation X and the new Millennial into the workplace, whose expectations of work are markedly different to those of their predecessors. Armed with sophisticated mobile technology and increasingly freed of geographic constraints, younger workers and those about to enter the workplace are rejecting long hours and permanent employment in favour of contracting, freelance work, frequent job moves and frequent career changes', Joanna Bawa states in *Business First*. One of the interesting points here is how those who need the new generation of workers to help propel their business forward will adapt as it's no longer about a 5% bonus after a hard year, a handful of luncheon vouchers or a slap on the back. Motivating workers going forward will be about emotional attachment, flexibility of attitude, and non-monetary reward for their involvement.

* What's your next online event? If the answer is 'what are you talking about', then it might be time to find out.

* 'The first printed books imitated handwritten manuscripts. The first photographs were portraits. Many early motion pictures captured theatrical plays on screen. So it's not surprising that in the late 1990s, companies tried hard to recreate their familiar business

environments online.' David Siegel, *Futurize Your Enterprise*.

* Spiders can bite – spiders are programmes that underpin a search engine's method of finding out what is available on the Internet. These programmes pick up on words and code to make an assessment of relevance and then rank sites on the basis of what they find. Spider technology changes as the companies behind them seek to refine and re-establish their footprint. The more you find out about them and how they change their search patterns over time, the better chance you have of getting noticed on the net.

* Contribute to the story – in the late 1990s, Amazon asked a writer called John Updike to participate in a networking experience. He wrote a few opening paragraphs for a book and posted it on Amazon, asking people to contribute and thereby continue the story. There was a cash prize for the winner each day but the experiment would extend for a six weeks to see if users really wanted to get involved in this way. The results staggered all those involved, Updike received more than 250,000 submissions as it became quite clear that people love to play a part.

* Hitches online – Google's email service (gmail to its friends) was down for four hours, which affected around 127 million users worldwide. Google admitted it had no idea what caused its network to fall over. Technology can be prone to slight technical hitches and being prepared for crashes isn't a bad practice.

* *Taming Tigers* by Jim Lawless includes the following section, 'You are writing the story of your life. You must be, mustn't you? Who else can be holding the pen? If we have the good fortune to be healthy and to live in a free state rather than a dictatorship, we're pretty much writing the story. In the developed world, we have the privilege and luxury at this unique point in our history of being completely in charge of our own stories, with tremendous opportunity all around us. For economic benefit, yes, but also for intellectual, social, cultural and personal advancement and adventure. So why don't we use that privilege fully? We have a Tiger. All of us have a Tiger. The Tiger is the thing that stops us; roars at us when we consider doing something that will require us moving into unknown waters. We know we can justify intellectually why we do not move past the impasse. We can list the reasons why we should not do it. We never, of course, refer to it as our Tiger. We

never allow others to see that we are actually justifying a lack of action caused by fear. Fear of the unknown. Fear of getting it wrong.'

* Online press – Adam Parker is Chief Executive of Realwire Ltd and on the website freshbusinessthinking.com, he outlines his five tips for great online press releases:

1. Release titles should be short and snappy, yet informative, and attract a reader's interest. Remember that most, if not all, recipients will only ever see this element of the release in their email application.

2. Use multimedia to enhance your story. Try to include an image or other accompanying information whenever relevant or appropriate.

3. Use hyperlinks to benefit you and the readers of your news in a number of ways.

4. Include a 'Notes to Editors' or 'About' (the company) section at the bottom of the release.

5. Contact details should always be included so that any receiver of your news knows who to contact if they want more information.

9 **74 Ways to Get a Life**

Here is a stream of ideas and thoughts that have come from my many interviews with business people. Topics and subject matter range considerably as a response to the question of work–life balance. They have been asked to analyse what has made a difference for them and how they have reacted in making key decisions. This is what they say:

1) Get emotional – the best way to get people on your side is to share your vision, enthusiasm and excitement. It's infectious!

2) Job satisfaction – if you are not happy in your career look to change it as quickly as possible.

3) Straight line – the road to greater happiness, prosperity and balance is never a straight one.

4) Results only – any move towards a 'results only' culture, rather than length of time we spend at the desk, will be hugely positive.

5) Enlist help – whether we like it or not, we will be more successful if

we get others to help. The best teams are not those made of all the same types of people, they are a combination of different styles, skills and attitudes.

6) Be original – the best way to really stand out from the crowd is to propose something original.

7) Learning – the best leaders are the quickest learners.

8) Disruptive – many new and innovative ideas are seen as disruptive, so appropriate delivery is essential to gain acceptance.

9) Define success – without some kind of yardstick or measure, it's tough to know how well we might be doing or where we really want to be.

10) Flexible – try to build a little more workplace flexibility, both mentally and physically into your career each year.

11) Other worlds – many industries are massively inward-looking, and don't try things simply because their competitors haven't. Broaden the horizons by taking information from other sectors, countries and people to see what is becoming good and common practice elsewhere.

12) Challenge norms – if you don't challenge yourself or your company's behavioural traits, the customer might just get there first.

13) Underpay – the link between pay and overwork is all about aspiration.

14) Rules – don't always play by the rules, look at how to start creating new ones.

15) Belief – creativity can mean sticking to your guns to convince people but don't ever confuse this with hardball. We are not trying to get people's backs up, just make them aware of a new perspective.

16) Un-train – you may need to remove people's preconceptions, old practices and ideals to effect real change. The un-training process will be different for each individual but it will be worthwhile when they eventually begin to see the light.

17) Simplify – if things get difficult or confusing for whatever reason, simplify every aspect until it becomes clear.

18) Feeling lucky – business is not like a game of roulette – in the long-run we all have some good luck and bad luck; our success is down to the quality of our decisions.

19) Journey – try to enjoy the journey, every step of the way.

20) Barter – look into how to swap or barter things that you need. Not just a teabag for a bowl of sugar but valuable business goods

and services like marketing or IT support, sales contacts or labour.

21) Creative process – identify when you are at your most innovative and try to increase that time. Good ideas can come in the bath, over a glass of wine or whilst walking in a deserted place.

22) Magnet – become a magnet for new ideas by rewarding and fostering innovative thinking and helping people gain acceptance for their process.

23) Cut meeting times – have sessions where no-one is allowed to sit down, go to the toilet or get too comfortable.

24) Separation – try to avoid artificially separating your life into work and non-work. Most issues affecting your work will also influence people close to you and what you do with your social time.

25) The past – accept what is done is in the past and can't be changed.

26) Forward motion – like riding a bike, if we want to keep balance we need to keep moving.

27) Long hours – the longer we work and communicate with business colleagues, the more likely we are to lose the ability to socialise and integrate in the way we should do.

28) Opportunities – a simple way to define yourself is to list half a dozen things you have not yet done. This often tells us more about ourselves than the things we have ended up doing.

29) You Can't Be Serious – have a sense of humour and never take yourself too seriously.

30) Preference – build a list of your personal traits, business likes and dislikes plus instincts to better understand your reference points for decision making.

31) Starting with ourselves – we should all have a better understanding of our strengths, weaknesses, preferences and personality traits. This will give us an improved sense of why we make key decisions.

32) Purchasing – make buying decisions on quality and service, not solely on price, whenever possible.

33) Guilt – only good people feel guilty.

34) Adrenalin – if you like the rush and pace of work, inject something new that resets your clock.

35) No need to worry – a business problem is just a good decision waiting to be made.

36) Respect privacy – no matter who you are dealing with.

37) Financial health check – ideally put a meeting with an accountant or financial advisor in the diary to run through the

money side of your life.

38) Curiosity – many entrepreneurs are continually curious about new areas of commerce. This trait alone can keep us moving forward.

39) Transferable – have you added to your list of transferable skills in the last year?

40) Engagement – engage people rather than confront them.

41) Customer expectations – most businesses are experiencing a revolution in customer requirements and empowerment. We need to get ahead of this curve!

42) Happy – list those things that make you happy and spend more time doing them.

43) Read more – reading not only adds to our understanding and knowledge base, the whole process is liberating.

44) Web-centric – for any business problem, start by searching the Internet to get different perspectives and background information.

45) Never lie – it is no foundation for business (or life).

46) Reactive – try not to overreact when things go wrong. It just makes others jumpy and fearful of trying anything new.

47) Material possessions – usually give us a short-term boost but that is all. Most of these things don't actually make us happier or more fulfilled over time. Changing your lifestyle is better than changing the car and you'll feel good for longer.

48) Know your job – then do it well.

49) Turn off to turn on – try a weekend without computers or mobiles. It will give you time to do new things, clear the mind and not just react.

50) Money, money, money – we can all be better with cash and small steps over time make a real difference. Try to give yourself maximum flexibility in financial dealings as circumstances usually change.

51) Keep your ear close to the ground – at all times.

52) When problems arise or mistakes get made, never get personal – there is no benefit.

53) Re-thinking – add originality and innovation, aesthetics and novelty, imagination and freshness to what you do.

54) Risk – the commercial decisions we make on a day-to-day basis carry an element of risk so we need to try to offset some of this until we feel comfortable.

55) Be one of the positive people – those that others want to hang

out with.

56) Under-promise and over-deliver – whenever you can.

57) Understand your mood swings – work out what gets you back on the positive side again.

58) When your body talks – it's time to listen.

59) Blurred lines – the communication revolution has blurred lines between personal, private and work time. Many of us need to reestablish how and when we are available to work.

60) Don't try to be perfect – just be effective.

61) Information flow – try to improve the flow of information getting to you in the office by looking at the quality of your relationships.

62) Take stock – on a regular basis, find some quiet time to evaluate where you are and how things are panning out.

63) Digest and understand others' points of view – before you dismiss them.

64) Network – try to regularly refresh and build your business network.

65) Know when enough is enough – we are all used to putting our foot down on the accelerator so find an aspect of your life when we need to stop pushing.

66) Downsize aspects of your life – especially the bits that sit on the wrong side of your happiness balance.

67) Take a pay cut – look at trading a pay cut against your own important lifestyle criteria, perhaps a shorter working week, more holidays or less corporate travel.

68) Get a mentor – or consider becoming a mentor.

69) Allergy – check to see if you have developed any allergies or intolerances. As we get older, things can slow us down.

70) Develop diversity in work – let people with different experiences, points of view and approaches share your vision.

71) Internet interface – most of us need an online interface to do business in some way so try to make it intuitive to use, different, memorable and get the user to leave feeling they have had a personal experience.

72) Prioritise – decide what is really important to you and get those things in some kind of order.

73) Instinct – trust your gut feeling.

74) If you can't be happy – you might as well be downright grumpy!

Finally, if you have a new business idea or workplace issue and think I might be able to help, please visit my website jimbanting.com or email me on jimbanting@gmail.com. I would also like to hear any thoughts you have on work–life elements that have worked for you. Good luck.

About the Author

Jim is a marketer, producer, graphic designer, innovative thinker and serial entrepreneur. He has a diverse range of commercial interests and companies, from creative services to property, journalism to e-tailing. He has blue chip business training, experience of working in a number of countries and a list of clients that includes household names. He is a regular writer for Golf Asia magazine and invests in many start-up ventures.

Jim enjoyed a fast-track career at Virgin, Philips Media and the Hollywood film studio, Metro-Goldwyn-Mayer before setting-up his own business at the age of 35 years. He continues to be a highly energetic, innovative and respected businessman, working from his central London office.

He was born in Exeter, Devon and has homes in Surrey and London.